Banjara Tribe of Kalahandi
Culture, Rituals and Religion

Banjara Tribe of Kalahandi
Culture, Rituals and Religion

Dr. Geetanjali Panda

Delta Book World
New Delhi-110 002

ISBN: 978-93-85719-17-2
First Published in 2021

Published by **Abhishek Goel** on behalf of

Delta Book World
G-4, Prahlad House
4832/24, Ansari Road
New Delhi - 110 002 (India)

Tel.: 011-4707 2321
E-mail: deltabookworld@gmail.com
Website: www.kaveribooks.com

PRINTED IN INDIA

Dedicated to

My Only Brother Debasish

ACKOWLEDGEMENT

I would like to express my gratitude to Dr. Sabita Acharya, Prof. P.G. Department of Anthroplogy, for her help and prepare the field training programme at Koksara block of Kalahandi district.

I express my heart felt gratitude and thanks to Dr. Jagannath Dash, Retd Prof. of Anthroplogy, for his help, guidance and advice during the field work for this work.

I am very much obliged to the inhabitants of the villages Dabriguda and Hanspada, for their help and cooperation in obtaining the required data.

I express my thanks to the B.D.O. and staff of Koksara block for their support and cooperation in the overall improvement of this book.

Lastly, I extend by sincere thanks to my husband Mr. Ashok Kumar Acharya for his helping hand. To all my well-wishers especially Dr. Subodh Kumar Mohanty who helped me a lot, I delightfully acknowledge my gratitude.

Dr. Geetanjali Panda

PREFACE

Religion is always based upon beliefs and rituals. For both primitive and modern people, religious activities are usually based on clan based beliefs and rituals. This book focuses on major variables of religion. The book presents an interpretation of the data collected on the topic of Banjara Tribe of Kalahandi: Culture, Rituals and Religion.

The first chapter has been dedicated to an introduction to the problem of study, theoretical background, and methods and techniques of data collection.

The second chapter has been dedicated to people and area, geographical distribution, flora and fauna, road communication, census analysis and Banjara culture of the people at a glance.

The third chapter discusses the Banjara Gods and Spirits.

The fourth chapter discusses the annual cycle of festivals and rituals, their importance and functions among Banjara people.

In the fifth chapter, basic spheres of a human life-cycle among the Banjara people like birth, marriage and death and the ritual for such occasions have been discussed.

The sixth chapter discusses the various religious functionaries like priest, medicine man, doctor etc. along with their changing status and role.

The seventh chapter discusses the world view of Banjara people.

The eighth chapter discusses religion and the changes in practices of the Banjara people due to the advent of other religions and various other factors. The last chapter focuses on the findings of the study, along with the view of the investigator and conclusion of the study.

CONTENTS

1

INTRODUCTION

> "Religion is the virtue by which men show God due worship and reverence" – *Thomas Aquinasi*

The word 'Religion' has been derived from the Latin root word *"Religio"* which means, *"to bind"*. It may be interpreted as to bind man and supernatural beings together. Tylor has presented the most minimum definition of religion as *"the belief in supernatural beings"*. He mentioned animism as the central theme of it, which is the basis of all religions. In former sense, the implication is the belief in and observation of sign of divine communication. In latter sense, the implication is the performance of necessary action, which may bind to get man and supernatural elements together. Both the implications and their relevance reveal that beliefs and rituals have been found to be the main components or parts of all religions everywhere.

The religious institutions in non western societies are more closely interrelated with the rest of the lives of the westerners, than they are in our own society, making it difficult, if not impossible, to study any aspect of their life without touching upon their religious behavior. So to draw a broad idea about the primitive people we have to first study about their religious institutions. Now due to the advent of modernization, we use various advanced technologies, due to which we remove more from nature than our ancestors. Therefore, our religious institutions reflect this distance by becoming more secularized. The effect that religion has on moulding economic, political, legal and other social institutions is therefore minimized. The variety of agricultural practices and the reasons behind them don't undergo many changes from one culture to another due to ecological conditions and environmental factors. In contrast with the religion the variation is almost unlimited. Anything within the realm of the human imagination is possible and where we have scientific answers for the *"why"* in agriculture, and we have no such answers for the *"why"* in religion.

Thus, religion, whether primitive or modern, is based on beliefs and rituals. Rituals consist of certain observances on a sacred day or days that are considered important for a certain group of people. These observances may be positive or negative which imply action and abstention. Beliefs are characters of the rituals and also a rationalization of the same. But the anthropological approach to the study of religion will not limit our attention to such beliefs and rituals, for it also include the various ideas that people make about other forces in the universe, and the place of man in nature and the practices that people carryout in an attempt to control their environment. In our society we differentiate religion from magic and science. But in primitive societies, these tend to be fused together and it is difficult for the observer to separate them. Primitive people do not have technological ability to control their environment. Therefore, they mainly depend upon religion and magic.

So Religion and magic play a great role in the lives of primitives. They learn religious beliefs as they grow up, and they develop understanding about them as a part of their culture. So religion is culturally universal in nature. The French sociologist Emile Durkheim, emphasized three aspects of religions;

1. The social context of religious system;
2. The sacred aspect of religion;
3. The moral basis of religion in society;

(John friedl and John E.Preiffer, 1977:427)

The real purpose of religion as given by Durkheim is to express people's beliefs about the Universe. Religion structures the universe and puts things in order, relates what is unknown to what is known. Bronislaw Malinowski pointed out that the nature of the social order is justified in the myths that people create and believe in. Thus, myths explain why the world is the way it is and why it should remain that way. As part of the system of beliefs about the nature of the universe, religion offers a guide to behavior among people, including a system of rules they must follow.

Religion fulfills basic and universal human needs, by enabling people to cope with the unknown and uncontrollable. But in the United States, religion has become more secular in nature. The concept of Soul and after Life are the primary concerns of religion, replacing problems, such as climate, illness and soon. Social life must be based upon rules of behavior. Religion can provide those rules so that human interaction can be based upon predictable responses and the expectation of certain patterns of behavior. Religion plays a role in guiding our investigations and helps us from falling into our own cultural trap, thus becoming subjective in our analysis of non-western religious behavior. According to Geertz's definition however, any system of belief may be characterized as religion. Religion serves to offer answer which can't always be explained by the sciences. So sciences also accept that everywhere there is God.

The Religion or conception of nature of the supernatural differs from society to society and people to people. For some the supernatural may be constituted as a ghost or spirit, for others if may be an impersonal power which pervades everything in this world. For another group of people, it may be manifested through a pantheon of anthro-pomorphic and Goddesses or a single high God and so on. So it can be safely said that it was a result of religion that an ancient society came to be constituted on the basis of the family, agnatic lineages and the clans with its law of succession, property, authority and marriage. In the factions of religion, S.F. Nadel states that religion is an effective instrument for social integration.

Life on the earth is full of sorrow and miseries and not a happy gay affair of togetherness as one would like to believe. There are uncertainties in life. Our ambitions and hopes are sometimes not fulfilled. In these circumstances religion also helps us in achieving the psychological adjustments and peace of mind. So religion helps in the building of morality among individuals. In every society religion has a great role to play. It holds together societies and sustains their structure. It also provides individuals with specific experiences and stimulation. So religion is said to be born out of physical and social needs. When we face any difficult situation or our mental equilibrium is imbalanced, we seek the help of supernatural elements to overcome crisis in life. The study of religion is important and essential because it helps indirectly to solve some social and economic problems of society. Religion has a role in rationalizing and justifying the ultimate group needs. It acts as an agent of social control by providing rewards for the good and punishment for the bad.

Religion and art complete the adjustment of man to this universe by providing him with security against forces that are more powerful than him. So Religion aids in social survival.

DEFINING RELIGION

The main characteristics of religion may be described in terms of *'nine meanings':*

> 'The primary meaning' of religion is the experience of God, communion with and love and praise of him.
>
> 'The second' meaning is man's experience of himself as a mind not to be identified with the body or any portion of it.
>
> 'The third' meaning is in accepting and interpreting nature as created by God and responding to it as instrumental to the purposes of God for men in the ideals. He reveals to them.
>
> 'The fourth' meaning is the sharing in social life, not primarily as a result of biological processes or for secular benefits, but as a fundamental of the religious ideal.
>
> 'The fifth' meaning is the experience of peace, joy and bliss in the communion of men as minds with God as mind.
>
> 'The sixth' meaning is the acceptance of saintliness, moral goodness, truth and beauty in all their forms, as divinely intended for men.
>
> 'The seventh' meaning in the individual's consciousness of

> defect, especially of sin, together with an awareness of the way of salvation and at least in part an experience of salvation.
>
> 'The eighth' meaning is the attitude towards suffering.
>
> 'The ninth' meaning is the conviction of spiritual continuity beyond death; the aspiration to, the hope, for the faith in eventual attainment of happiness. *(A.G. Widgery)*

'Religion is Divine spirit's knowledge of itself through the mediation of finite spirit. The object of religion is the same as that of philosophy eternal truth in its own objectivity, God and nothing but God and the explication of God.' *(Hegel)*

The opxinions quoted here seem to have this is common, that they would define religion primarily by its reference to supernatural objects.

Religion is an emotion resting on a conviction of a harmony between ourselves and the universe at large'. *(J.M.E. McTaggart)*

'A Religion, on its doctrinal side, can thus be defined as a system of general truths which have the effect of transforming character when they are sincerely held and vividly apprehended. Religion is the art and the theory of the internal life of men, so far as it depends on the man himself and on what is permanent in the nature of things. Religion is what the individual does with his own solitariness. Collective enthusiasm, revivals, institutions, churches, rituals, bibles, codes of behavior are the trappings of religion, it's passing from.' *(Alfred North Whitehead)*

'Religion is the sign of the oppressed creature, the feeling of a heartless world; the soul in a place within soul. It is the opium of the people.' *(Karl Marx)*

In these definitions, religion is defined primarily based in terms of the beliefs, experiences or psychological states of human beings.

'The real characteristic of religious phenomena is that they always supposed a bipartite division of the whole universe, know and knowable division of the whole universe, know and knowable into classes which embrace all that exists, but which radically exclude each other. Sacred things, those to which the interdictions protect and isolate, profane things to which those interdictions are applied and which must remain at a distance from the first.' *(Emile Durkheim)*

A religion is a unified system of beliefs and practices related to any sacred thing, that is to say, forbidden beliefs and practices or things set apart as important from the ordinary activities, which unite, into one single community, like for example, a church and followers are all those who adhere to them.

Religion can be defined as 'The set of beliefs which postulate and seek to regulate the distinction between an empirical reality and a related and significant supra-empirical segment of reality; the language and symbols which are used in relation to this distinction; and the activities and institutions which are concerned with its regulation.' *(Michael Hill)*

In this definition, religion is defined in terms of its effects or demands on human behavior and on social institutions.

'It is emphatically true that the first traceable conception of a supernatural being is the conception of the ghost, and from the ghost once uniformly conceived, have arisen the variously conceived, supernatural beings. We thus reach the conclusion that ancestor worship is the root of every religion.' *(Herbert Spencer)*

Religion has played a strategic part in the human enterprise of world building. Religion implies the farthest reach of man's self externalization, of his infusion of reality with his own meanings.

'Religion implies that human order is projected into the totality of being. Put differently, religion is the audacious attempt to conceive of the entire universe as humanly significant.' *(P.L. Berger)*

One can derive from the numerous definitions of religion that in order to find out the nature and function of religion, a thorough research into the origin of religion is first required.

'In the totality of human experiences and activities the religious phenomenon presents itself as irreducible to any other category save its own and as definitely and always belonging to its own category and no other'. *(J. Goetz)*

Religion is one thing to the anthropologist, another to the sociologist, another to the psychologist and another again to the next psychologist, another to the Marxist, another to the mystic, another to the Zen Buddhist and yet another to the Jew or the Christian. As a result, there are a great variety of anthropological, sociological, psychological, naturalistic and religious theories of the nature of religion. There is consequently, no universally accepted definition of religion and quite possibly there never will be.' *(John Hick)*

'The fact of the matter is that the definition of religion

is in principle impossible, if by definition we mean the distinction of one object or group of objects from other objects or groups in the same class. This is the famous and classical use of definition per genus it differentiation, [i.e. according to general class and specific difference which is the basis of all scientific classification. But in the case of the ultimate, the self, the world and God, this type of definition does not apply for there is no known class and no distinction within that class'. *(L. W. Grensted)*

In these groups there is an agreement that the activities and phenomena described as *'religious'* are so disparate that no satisfactory definition can include them all. *(Reference taken from Francis clark, 1981: 12-17)*

Loisy justifies his selection of sacrificial rites as the subject of his analysis of religion by saying that rites are in all religions the most stable and lasting element and consequently that is which can best discover the spirit of ancient cult. In primitive religion there is only philosophical speculation.

Robert Smith states that in this connection with every religion, whether ancient or modern, we find on the one hand, certain beliefs, and on the other, certain institutions ritual practices and rules of conduct. Religion was a body of fixed traditional practices to which every member of society conformed as a matter of course.

Redfield Brown suggested another formula that Religion is everywhere, an expression in one form or another, of sense of dependence on a power outside or in within ourselves, which we may speak of as spiritual or moral power.

In the *Introduction to the History of Religion* by F.B.

Jevons, religion for him is an evolutionary development from totemism, animism being rather a primitive philosophical theory than a form of religious belief to polytheism to monotheism.

According to Durkheim "A religion is a unified system of beliefs and practices relative to sacred things, that is to say things set apart and forbidden beliefs and practices which unite into one single moral community called a church, all those who adhere to them". (W.A. Lessa, 1958: 07-09)

Tribal Religion

Tribal religion is otherwise called as primitive religion in some anthropological literature. The term 'primitive' suggests 'backward' societies that show under development in the evolutionary scale.

E.B. Tylor writes that primitive religion was rational, it arose from observation, in adequate and from logical deduction from them, however faulty, that it constituted a crude material philosophy.

According to Marett, primitive people have a feeling that there is an occult power in certain people andthings and it is the presence or absence of this feeling which cuts off the sacred from the profane. It gives rise to taboo to separate the two worlds from one another that is wonder world and work a day world, and this feeling or emotion of awe, a compound fear, wonder, interest, and respect and even love, whatever evokes this emotion is treated as a mystery i.e religion. According to Andrew Lang, primitive people believe that the world around them must have been made by a superior being. It is not a later development from the ideas of ghost and soul or anything else.

Durkheim's analysis says that early religion lacked creeds and dogmas but consisted of entirely religious institutions and practices. Rites are connected with myth but myths do not explain rites. If this is so, then we must seek for an understanding of primitive religion, in its rituals and analyse a basic rite in ancient religion, that of sacrifice. Sacrifice is a general institution in primitive religion. He also said tribal religion is idealized on the Gods. The great God is implying the synthesis of all the clans represented in them.

In the last half of 19th century, Robertson Smith asserted that the religion of primitive people developed out of the relation between a community and its Gods who were seen as fair and benevolent. According to Dr. Majumdar, tribal religion has occupied the position between magic and religion, between pseudo science and science. The tribals pray to the spirits proceeding over diseases such as small-pox and cholera spirits, dwelling in rock and hill tops, hunting trees and rivers. All the happenings are properly propitiated towards of the dangers associated with the belief in malevolent and benevolent spirits and powers which regulate the destiny of man. Dr. Hutton has remarked that tribal religions are not sufficiently represented as it were surplus material not yet built into the temple of Hinduism.

All of tribal religion is associated with animism. But it is not the whole truth. Yet, E.B. Tylor has applied the term 'animism' for primitive people. It was of great importance to him since it characterized tribes very low in the scale of humanity and then ascended into deeply modified transmission, but from first to last retaining an unbroken continuity in the modest of highly civilized and cultured people. The theories of animism based on two aspects:

1. The souls of individuals, capable of continued existence after the death of the body.
2. The second concerning other spirits, upward to the rank of powerful deities.

After going through all these factors, we can conclude that primitive people mainly believed the life after death, they also believed in polytheism due to which they worshipped and continue to worship different deities for different purposes, they also believe in animatism by which they worship hills, trees, water etc. The tribal religion is heavily based on beliefs and rituals.

Theoritical Framework

Anthropology, sometimes described as the whole study of man, is a science that has become more and more specialized and compartmentalized into sub-disciplines. There is prehistoric anthropology, psychological anthropology and linguistic and cultural anthropology. Traditionally anthropology has tended to concentrate on small communities and especially on the customs of men in such societies. Religious customs rites, beliefs, religious conventions and religious sanctions for kinship and community relation are central in such tribal societies. Consequently anthropological studies have shown much light on religion in primitive and simple communities and have provided a vast field of data on which theories about the nature of religion can be based. For those who would explain religion itself by explaining how it must have originated in the life of prehistoric man, the anthropology of primitive societies is of paramount importance in their study of religion. *[Francis Clark, 1981: 47-48]*

From etymological point of view, religion is derived

from the word "religion" which means, "bond". Religion is a Latin word. Various theories have been formed on religion.

Philosophy of Religion

It is customary to trace the Philosophy of Religion back to Plato. The Philosophy of Religion is concerned with many questions such as existence and nature of God; questions about ultimate being and about the contingency and dependence of the finite world; questions about the existence of soul after death, questions about moral law.

For the philosophers in the metaphysical tradition, philosophy of religion means the use of man's reason to raise questions about ultimate reality and to discuss philosophic-theological issues. For many post Kantian philosophers, it means a philosophical criticism of human feelings or sentiments and language described as religious. The work of philosophy of religion is to expose the meaninglessness of religious language. Otherwise it is an inquiry into the application of religious discourse. So the religious discourse is a self-enclosed language system which can't validate any reference beyond itself. So at least it can be said that the status of religious language has a central role in the modern discussions of religion. *(Francis Clark, 1981:48)*

Sociology of Religion

Where anthropologists have concentrated their studies on tribal societies, religious sociologists tend to investigate the role of religion in more complex and developed societies. As a discipline, the sociology of religion may be said to have arisen as a reaction against too narrow individualistic explanations of the origins and nature of religion as given by Tylor and Frazer. These authors proposed that religious ideas and observances were the conclusion to a process of reasoning in the mind of primitive man, seeking a rational answer to the problems and mysteries of his short and dangerous life. *(Francis Clark, 1981: 48)*

According to Tylor, religion had been regarded as a product of civilization. He states that primitive societies have their own religious activity which is not very different from civilized societies. His theory traces on the idea of said rather than ghost. It mainly interests in two theseis, first accounting for its origin and second for its development. Tylor said dreams gave birth to soul and soul gave way for the existence of spirit. Tylor said primitive religion was rational. It arose from observation, from adequate and logical deductions, however faulty, that it constituted a crude material philosophy. For the conduct of daily life man has evolved various humanisms. Thus there are his responses to himself i.e. to his own biological needs, and bring him into particular contact with his natural environment. This relationship that exists between human beings necessitated by the need to organize is made possible by language education, social organization and political organization. So it can be said that religion is also the human response to the apprehension of something on power, which is supernatural or supersensory.

The above is a short description of Tylor's theory. But Tylor's contribution has led to another famous author's contribution - Frazer's contribution.

According to Frazer mankind are everywhere and sooner or later goes through three stages of intellectual development from magic to religion and from religion to science which he may have taken over from Comte's phases - the theological, the metaphysical and the positive. The conclusion gave by him is based on Australian data that the simpler the culture, the more the magic and the less the religion. Australian tribe has animistic and theistic beliefs and culture and magic in their culture is less. (E.E. Evanspritchard 1971: 26-29)

Emile Durkheim and his associates stressed that religion was first and foremost social phenomenon. He emphasized on the functions of religion in society. It was an expression and a solution to social needs. Religion emerged in prehistory as an expression and lubricant for social relations, not as the answer to a mental problem.

Durkheim was influenced by Fustel-de-Coulanges, and Robertson Smith. They were putting forward a structural theory of the genesis of religion that religion arises out of the very nature of primitive society. Durkheim's analysis said that early religion lacked creeds and dogmas, but consisted of entirely religious institutions and practices. Rites are connected with myth but myths do not explain rites. If this is so, then we must understand that primitive religion is in its ritual and since basic rite in ancient religion is that of sacrifice. Sacrifice is a general institution is primitive religion. He said religion is social and an objective.

Religion arises out of nature of social life itself, being in the simpler societies bound up with other facts, law, economics and art. Which later separate out from it and lead their own independent existences. Besides Religion is the way in which a society sees itself as more than collection of individuals and by which it maintains its solidarity and ensures its continuity. Once brought into existence by collective action, religion gains a degree of autonomy and proliferates in all sorts of ways which can't be explained by reference to the social structure which gave birth to it but only in terms of other religious and other social phenomena in a system of its own. Durkheim emphasizedon four cardinal ideas taken from Robert Smith that primitive religion is a clan cult and that cult is totemic, the god of the clan is the clan itself divinized, and that totemism is the most elementary or primitive and in that sense original form of religion known to us. *(E.E. Evanspritchard, 1971:55)*

He also gave a concept totemism which are divined for the most part, not at all imposing, and just humble little creature like ducks, rabbits, and frogs and worms whose intrinsic qualities could scarcly have been the origin of the religious sentiment they inspired. It derived from the word totem; it is the symbol of both God and vital principle of society.

For Durkheim religion belongs to a broader class, the sacred, everything real and ideal belonging to one of two opposed classes the profane and the sacred. Taboo is also given importance. Religious beliefs are the representations which express the nature of sacred things and rites are the rules of conduct which prescribe how a man should comfort himself in the presence of sacred objects. Here he proposed both magic and religion as sacred. Here, he treated religion as a group affair, something collective. *(Ibid., 1971:56)*

Religion is thus a system of ideas by which individuals represent to themselves the society to which they belong and their relation with it. For Durkheim God is society. So there are certain rites ceremony only to awaken certain ideas and sentiments to attach the present to past and the individual to the group.

Max Weber another author, who was more interested in developed societies and economic factors, held that it was religion which brought about particular social groupings. These two alternative concepts associated with Durkheim and Weber were the main basis of sociological theory. *(Francis Clark, 1981:49)*

In due course, the sociology of religion became wide spread and accepted by most anthropologists. A.R. Raddiffe-Brown was another supporter of sociological theory of religion. He mainly concentrated on Durkheim's concept and said totemism arises from the general attitude when social segmentation takes place. He said, since religion has the function of maintaining the solidarity of society, it must vary in forms with types of social structure. In society with a linkage system we may expect to find ancestor cults.

Psychology of Religion

In sociological interpretation of religion there seemed a lack of mental, emotional and ideological aspects of religion. In the tradition of Schleiermacher (cf. Smart, pp 619-21), they concentrated on the feelings, hopes, fears, yearnings, institutions and other subjective states of believers. William and James gave wide currency to the notion that there are two basic kinds of religious outlook. The 'religion of the sick soul', which seeks salvation form sin and from cosmic evil, and 'religion of healthy mindedness', which is optimistic and affirms cosmic good. *(Ibid.1981:51)*

Both Spencer's theory of animism, ancestor worship and Tylor's theory of animism might be regarded as two various dream theory of the origin of religion. (E.E. Evanspritchard 1971:25)

Sigmund Freud turned his attention not only to the underlying motivation of religious beliefs and emotions of individuals in his own day, but also to the psychic origin of the religious ideas of early man.

Freud said, in his thesis that children both love and hate their parents, the son, deep in his unconscious wanting to kill the father and possess the mother (oedipus complex) and the daughter, deep in hers, wanting to kill the mother and be possessed by the father (the Electra complex). Religion is an illusion and Freud's book is called as, *"the future of an illusion",* (Ibid. 1971:42)

According to Herbert Spencer, primitive men are rational and given his small knowledge, his inferences are reasonable, if weak. He said rude people have no idea of natural explanation, as though they could have conducted various practical pursuits without it and other things can be dual way, but not man himself – the idea of duality given by him. He said the origin of religion is belief in ghost than in soul. The soul has temporary after life which is the appearance of the dead in dreams, so long as the dead are remembered and the first traceable conception of supernatural is that of a ghost. This gives importance of an indwelling ghost or spirit. Spencer said that the idea of ghost inevitably developed into that of gods, the ghosts are of remote ancestors or of superior persons becoming divinities and food and drink placed on their graves to please the dead becoming sacrifices and libation to the gods to propitiate them. So he gave the idea that ancestor worship is the root of every religion. (Ibid. 1971: 23-24)

Malinowski suggested that religion is universal because it is a response to anxieties and uncertainties that affect individual personally and as a consequence threaten to disrupt the social group. Today the psychology of religion can lay little claim to being a unified discipline. The inquirer is confronted with a bewildering aray of conflicting theories. There seem be almost as many psychologies of religion as there are psychologists of religion.

Concept Used

Religion: It is basically a belief system, which includes myths that explain the social and spiritual order and rituals through which the members of the religious community carry out their beliefs and act out the myths to explain the unknown.

Magic: It is the attempt to manipulate the forces of nature to derive certain desired results.

Science: A system of beliefs bases on observed relationship in the knowable universe and an attempt to manipulate natural forces based on experiment.

Mana: Inherent in the notion of animism is the concept of power. Furthermore, it is a special kind of power that can not be controlled because it is supernatural in origin. It can only be observed and in some cases manipulated but not created or destroyed. Belief in such power is characteristic of many different religious systems and anthropologists used Mana to denote it in its various forms.

Taboo: A supernatural prohibition against a specific behaviour or pattern, punishable by supernatural sanctions.

Animism: A religion belief in which a spirit or soul is attributed to all living things and sometimes is extended to in animate objects. The spirits are worshipped and at times, thought to have supernatural power.

Diviner: A religious specialist who is able to foresee future events or uncover the causes of past events. Divination reflects an attempt to control the forces of the universe through the prediction of future events.

Law of Contact or Contagion: A principle in the use of magic, stating that the things that have been in contact with each other continue to exert an effect on each other after they have become separated. (Also known as contagious magic).

Law of Similarity: A principle in the use of magic that involves manipulation of symbolic objects to produce the same effect upon an actual person.

Myth: A sacred story that serves as an explanation for the natural environment, a group's relationship to the supernatural or spirit world and their cultural customs and rituals. In non-literate societies these elaborate stories are part of an oral tradition passed on from one generation to the next and they function as guidelines to explain how and why rituals are performed.

Profane: Those aspects of society that are considered ordinary, having no special religious significance.

Religious Specialist: A position held in society by the individual considered most skilled in relating to the supernatural. Depending on the society, the position may be filled by a person who has undergone specialized training, or by a person considered to have inherited ability.

Rite of passage: A ceremony marking the change from one period or stage of life into another (also called life crises rite).

Ritual: A prescribed way of carrying out a religious activity, such as a prayer, an act of worship or a sacrifice. Rituals reinforce the belief system of a society and function both in terms of spiritual value and symbolic meaning for the group.

Sacred: Those aspects of the society that are considered special and are thought of as having a certain mystical quality.

Secularization: The process by which a society becomes more reliant on civil attitudes and explanations, rather than religious attitudes explanations.

Shaman: A religious specialist, considered to have contact with spirits and whose powers come directly from the supernatural forces. Communication with spirits usually takes place through possession and the individual serves as a medium of contact for the rest of the group.

Spirit possession: A religious practices involving the transmission of supernatural power through a human agent. The ritual occurs in a group situation in which a person becomes possessed by a spirit through trance, induced by drugs or some physical activity and then acts as a medium through which the spirit communicates to other people.

Superstition: A belief based on supernatural explanations, but with less conviction than a religious belief.

Totemism: A religious system based on the concept of totem which maybe an animal, a plant or a natural inanimate object signifying the symbolic unity of a group.

Witch Craft: An explanation of how or why certain events occurred. Witch-craft functions as an outlet for aggression and hostility, resolves tension and conflicts, explains otherwise inexplicable events and acts as a mechanism of social control by regulating behavior of certain members of society.

The book is based on the following aims and objectives:

The *first* aim is to highlight the culture of Banjara people in general. The way they dress themselves, their customs, their language system, their house pattern, their social institution etc., I would like to mark very vividly.

Second aim is to know the various supernatural concepts and powers associated with the Banjara's religious practices. While collecting various supernatural concepts of Banjara people, I also plan to collect their beliefs related to sacred objectsand trees, sacred birds and places, factors of purity and pollution along with associated social taboos and myths.

Third objective is to know the different types of festivals and religious rituals, which are observed by Banjara people. The data which I shall collect will mostly reflect various restriction and taboos associated with their festivals and religious rituals. This may show that a relationship always exists with the supernatural power and the observation of several festivals and rituals.

Fourth objective is to study the observances of pollution period and purity by Banjara people during their life cycle ritual. The Banjara people consider birth, puberty, marriage and death as the turning point of an individual's life.

Fifth, the subsequent objective is to know the role of different religious and magical specialists and their influences upon the Banjara people. The different types of spirits, how they are controlled by the magicians/sorcerers and also by religious specialists is also another aim of this study.

Sixth, further desire to know the world view of Banjara people, which will help to explore the Banjara configuration and religious perceptions.

Seventh, as no culture is static, the major objective of the study is to highlight the changing frontiers of Banjara religion, so that the present state of Banjara religion can be very well assessed.

In order to collect data, I went to Kalahandi (Koksora) for twenty-eight days to study the life-style of the Banjara people, living among them. For collection of data there must be followed some sort of methods or techniques, which are mainly followed by an Anthropologist.

These methods and techniques are given below;

(1) Observation of both participant and non participant as condition permitted.

(2) Interview method as both structured and unstructured, for both individual and group.

(3) Filling of the forms of preliminary census for each unit giving vital statistics about social structure.

(4) Memory recall method was not very useful and genealogy method was used for dieting memory lapses.

(5) People were ashamed and hesitated to answer questions such as puberty ritual, pregnancy period, different types of magic and witchcraft etc. This problem was tried to overcome by cross checking method.

Participant observation: When the observer participates with the activities of the group under study, it is known as participant observation. So, to collect data on festivals ceremonies and rituals I have very much applied the method of participant observation.

In Banjara society, usually the women both married and unmarried experience a lot of restriction in the field of their interaction with outsiders. At the time of worship, they do not allow the girls/ladies to go inside their "Devata Ghar". Inspite of that I have tried my best to take part in all worship. By doing participant observation, I can know the natural behavior of Banjara people. I became much close to them when I danced with their ladies. In every society the people always welcome a participant observer than a non-participant observer.

Non-participant observation: When the observation occurs without the participation in the activities of the group, it is called as non-participant observation. In this observation, the observers observe from adistance. In this work in case of death rituals, birth rituals, marriage ceremony observed form a distance.

Schedule: The schedule is the form containing some questions or blank tables which are to be filled by the workers after getting information from the informants. I have used schedules for the account of the belief in a variety of supernatural beings, the performances of ritual in the Banjara society, role of religious functionaries and other socio-economic importance. This helped me a lot in the analysis of all my data and to draw a general conclusion about the Banjara society.

Interview: According to Pauline Young "Interview may be regarded as a systematic method by which a person enters more or less imaginatively into the life of a comparative stranger". By interviewing, I can enter deeply into various situations and realize this significance of what the interviewee says. My informants are both male and female. Even though being a female student made communicating with males a bit awkward, I didn't face any such problems later on.

The rapport establishment is a very important factor in anthropological field study. To be a good researcher it is quite necessary to be a good rapport maker. For the first few days people are indifferent to us. To establish rapport among Banjara, we used various amicable terms with the informant and the Banjara people. At first sight we faced a lot of problem as the people looked upon us as strangers but later on they became very close to us when we shared our purpose for studying them. On the very first day we went to visit every household and started numbering the houses of the village for household census work. Initially they hesitated to allow for numbering the houses. After they carefully listened to our teacher and our purpose in general they all allowed us for numbering and didn't hesitate to give us information about people and the village.

The informants who have really helped me a lot are Chandrabhanu Naik (a young man), Kanchan Bala Naik (a married woman), Amika Naik (a widow), and Minakshi Naik (a 22 year old girl). Apart from these people, all the villagers have helped during the study.

While collecting data during field study I faced many difficulties, but still adjusted with these difficulties and went on collecting data. Firstly, the Banjara villages were far away from our boarding place. So I had to walk at least for 8 to 9 kilometers. So it was very difficult to communicate with them. Secondly, the Banjara language is a mixture of Hindi and Chattisgarhi. Perhaps it is quite easy for us to understand their language. But now they were speaking the local Oriya of Kalahandi, which is a bit difficult for me to understand if I asked any question to them. Thirdly, most of the Banjara people are very much co-operative only for one or two days. But as we started to visit continuously they started to avoid us and became bored of us. Fourthly, when I asked about their life-cycle rituals they did not take any interest to tell anything. They tried to avoid questions.

They are agriculturists and as the agricultural harvest was over so. They are free in the morning hour between 9-10 A.M., I usually found most of people in the village and got required data. Beside various difficulties, I tried my best to collect maximum data on Banjaras and later adjusted to our adversities and prepare this book.

2

PEOPLE, HABITAT AND CULTURE

The Banjara are found distributed in most parts of the Indian sub-continent except Sikkim, Nagaland, Mizoram, Meghalaya, Manipur and Arunachal Pradesh. In states like Andhra Pradesh, Bihar, Jharkhand, Maharastra and Orissa, they are included in the list of Schedule Tribes. Where as in the states like Haryana, Karnataka, Himalchal Pradesh, Punjab, Rajasthan, Chandigarh and Delhi they are included in the list of Scheduled Caste. In other states and Union Territories they are neither under ST nor SC list. In Union Territories like Andaman and Nicobar Island and Lakshadweep, they are not found. From the British records, it is found that they have about 31 synonymous names in different parts of India. They also have about12 caste or sub groups distributed in different parts of the country.

In Orissa, Banjaras are mostly found in the districts of Sambalpur, Kalahandi, Koraput and Balangir with a total population of 1925 according to 1981 Census. Banjaras are usually known as a Nomadic group of people who move from place to place in search of work. They use bullock carts for carrying the goods or commodities for trade. It is said that the name Banjara is derived from the Sanskrit root

'Banijaya Kara', a merchant. However, historically they are said to exit between 600-360 B.C. from India. Some historical evidences also say that they have gone beyond India and are found in European states especially in Italy with name "Lambard". However, Banjaras came to Orissa in 18th century and established their settlements in different parts of western Orissa as Nomadic communities. They migrated from Madhya Pradesh to close western Orissa as the place of their habitation. With the gradual conversion of forest land to agricultural land, they wanted to settle in some of their temporary settlement until they felt the basic living conditions are suitable with agriculture and permanent settlement. Usually it is found that most of the Banjara settlements are little away from the main region village. Mainly because as nomadic communities they were prefering to camp outside the village usually in an open field, and later on when they chose to settle with agriculture, they rightly chose their temporary sites as their permanent settlement. This is very much visible even now in most Banjara inhabited villages. Banjaras are very much now acquainted with Oriya. Though they speak very good Hindi and also Chattisgarhi, their mother tongue is "Gorgoli".

Thus, in nutshell, Banjaras have come to Orissan territory in tribes even though their living conditions are bit devoloped than the neighbouring tribes and non-tribes. In India they are mostly found in a greater concentration in Maharastra, Rajasthan, Madhya Pradeshand Andhra Pradesh.

GEOGRAPHICAL LOCATION

The study was undertaken at Koksara block among the Banjara people at different Banjara villages. The villages which were surveyed for data collection are Dabriguda,

Hanspada, Mushapalli and Sarasmal. These villages were also used for cross-checking the data. These areas are under the Koksara block of Kalahandi district. This place is 508 kms away from Bhubaneswar, capital city of Orissa. The village is 61 kms away from Bhavanipatna, the district headquater of Kalahandi. The study is mainly carried out in villages Dabriguda and Hanspada.

CLIMATE AND RAINFALL

The climatic condition of the village Dabriguda and Hanspada are almost same as that of the entire district. Kalahandi is situated in the North-Eastern corner of the Deccan plateau and is similar in many respects to the Deccan plateau. The year may be divided into four seasons. The hot season starts from March to May followed by South West monsoon from June to September. October and November constitute the past monsoon season. The cold season is from December to February. In the month of May the daily temperature is usually about 54 degrees celcius. It is the hottest month. Due to scarcity of rainfall, this area is called as drought affected area.

FLORA AND FAUNA

The flora and fauna of the village Dabriguda and Hanspada have quite interesting features. The nearby areas of the village are full of different varieties of plants and animals. The village Dabriguda and Hanspada comprise of animals like cows, bull, goats of different colour, docks, hen, cock, parrot, dogs, buffaloes and different types of snakes.

Secondly, the floras of these villages include drumsticks, mango, lily, guava, tamarind, berry, bamboo, papaya, bears (simba), sugarcane, cauliflower, cabbage, radish, kendu.

Sugarcane has been extensively cultivated. At the end of summer season until the beginning of winter season, paddy is grown in the farm lands. After the harvesting of paddy, Uraad dal is cultivated in the land.

ROAD AND COMMUNICATION

A kachha road runs into the village making lanes and by lanes. The kachha road of one village is connected with the foot-path of another village and finally all these inter-connected roads lead to the main road of the Koksara block. The roads of this village are made of hard mud and during the summers and winters, the surface of the road are full of fine particles of dust. But during the rainy season the roads becomes muddy and slippery. The village does not have any conveyance facility to Koksara block. To communicate with the neighbouring villages, they mostly use two wheelers, or they cover the distance on foot. They go to Bhawanipatna, Rigada, Jaipur and Navarangpur by bus which departs from Koksara bus stand.

The "Gountia" family of Dabriguda village have scooter and motor-cycle to travel from one place to another. Cycle is found in almost every household.

GEO-ETHNIC COMPOSITION

In village Dabriguda and Hanspada we found different groups of ethnic people like Banjara, Gond, Schedule Caste, Karana, Brahmin, Gouda etc. Banjara people are numerically more and Karana and Brahmin peoples are less with only one representative in Dabriguda village.

Mostly the people maintain good relationship with each other but it is very formal. The Gond and Schedule Caste have occupied a lower position than the Banjara people. On the occasion of marriage or any such ritual all the caste groups are invited but they don't take cooked food in any occasion. But they take rice and other cooking materials from the Banjara people during marriages as a gift. Banjara people are higher caste in social stratification from the Gond and Scheduled Castes.

CENSUS ANALYSIS (VILLAGE)

The total population of Dabriguda village constitute the Gond and Harijan. Harijans are more in number than other caste group. Their health status is not so good. So mortality is higher in aged groups than other age groups. Females are more illiterate than males.

In higher studies the number of male members are higher than female because female members are engaged in household works and they get little scope for higher studies.

The Banjara people practiced agriculture work as their primary occupation. The rest number of population is engaged in politics, in making cow dung and firewood collection. The highest number of males and females are working as daily wage laborers.

In the marital analysis, it is found that out of total Banjara population, 70 per cent are married and out of this 40 per cent males and 30 per cent females. The highest percentage of marriage among the females are seen during the age group of 16-20 years and 21 to 25 years among the males. The lowest number of marriage occur among Banjara in between age group of 26 to 30 years. Due to literacy and awareness among the Banjaras the age of marriage is increasing.

The Banjara people speak Gorboli and also know other languages such as Odia, Hindi and English. Some Gond people also know Banjara language. They speak Odia fluently because they live in Odisha and always talk with Odia people. They speak Hindi well because Gorbali is the mixture of Hindi and Chattisgarhi. They speak very less English because of low educational status.

The Banjara males and females have visited Dharmagarh for various purposes like marriage purposes, curing of diseases, marketing etc. Very few people are able to go to Uttar Pradesh, Chennai and Delhi for job purposes. Most of them have visited Bhubaneswar and Puri for religious purposes.

They have gone to Dharmagarh for marketing and other daily activities. Most of them go to Junagarh for marketing and other religious event. No Gond people go to Uttar Pradesh, Raipur, Jaypore, Brahmapura, Bhopal, Chennai and Malkangiri because of long distance.

From the Harijan group males and females have gone to Bhawanipatna for marketing and other purposes. Harijan people also did not go the Delhi, Brahmapur, Kolkata, Raipur and Jaipur due to high distance.

Among all the groups, most of the people have gone to Dharamgarh for different purpose and very few people have gone out of Odisha due to long distance. But now they are going to different cities outside Odisha insearch of jobs and extra-income.

The age sex composition of Banjara analysis shows that the members under age group (11-15) and (16-20) are high in the village under study. The total number of individuals are less, under the age group (56-60). So it is clear that their health status is not so good. So in the aged group mortality is higher.

From the marital status, it is seen that the Banjara and Gouda males are remaining more unmarried than the Harijans. The Goud males and females are more in number respectively than other caste group. The Harijan unmarried males are very low than the female.

ECONOMIC ORGANISATION

Economic organisation is a type of social action. It involves the combination of various kinds of human services with one another and non-human goods and services. The primary occupation of the Banjara people was mainly business. But now days they have adopted wet and upland cultivation. The wetland of Dabriguda village mainly belongs to "Gountia" family. So they are economically stronger than other villagers. They cultivate paddy of different varieties like Hasareek, Khandagiri, Parijat, Bandana. Bhattaswarna are modern seeds. But the traditional seeds are chingiri, Dasarmoti, Bareng, Momochi, Puagi, Chudi, Maipal, Balaji, Khujikular, Kalikhuji, Malapa, Goendi, Godakhuta, Magura, Gelei, Ratanachudi, Tendulia, Mahulkhuchi etc. The modern seeds are provided by different government development programmes for cultivation. They get the seeds, fertilizer and irrigation facility from co-operative society free of cost. They spend more than their income, for which they always live in a deficit budget, which affects their economy. The main cause of their deficit budget is in fooding and ritual expenditure.

Market: Market is a common place where buying and

selling of different commodities takes place. In Banjara society, market has a great role.The market takes place twice in a week such as in Koksara block onWednesday and in Majhiguda village on Sunday. The market place at Koksara block is very large in size but the market of Majhiguda village is quite small in size. They purchase their daily necessities from Koksara market and also sell their products such as Guava, Dry fish, Berry and clothes in the market. They never get proper price for their products because they use the traditional measuring devices. They are very much exploited by some of the non-tribal, which declines their economic status more and more. They buy other things in higher rates because of modern measuring devices.

They also work as wage labours when they get time from their cultivation. They get Rs. 45 per day in construction works. As the markets are situated very near to Banjara people, so when people come on Wednesday, they not only come to market not only for selling and buying purpose but also interact with their friends and close relatives.

RELIGIOUS ORGANISATION

The Banjara people are very religious in nature like Oriya people and they also celebrate many festivals. They worship 28 gods and goddesses. These gods and goddesses are worshipped in different rituals. The main gods and goddesses of this society are Banjari, Danteswari, Durputa, Taljabhabani, Taljakankali, Pir, Dula, Matrala, Meramaa, Lukudia, Basterein and Barsarmajhi.

The supreme deities of Banjara society are Danteswari, Taljabhabani, and Durputamaa. However, for all purposed of trade in the past they use Banjari Devi as the presiding deity.

In Banjara culture the main god and goddess are categorized on the basis of their hierarchy and power. Besides the worship of all these deities they observe various festivals like Dussehra, Holi, Diwali, Tij festivals, Charupuja, Hareliuansh, Rakhi purnima, Siva Ratri, Pausa Purnima, Pedrani Devi Jatara, Nabanna etc.

In the month of April-May they do not observe any festivals. In the month, July-August they observe Rakhipurnima, Tij festival and Hareliuansh. The "Tij festivals" is mainly observed for nine days and in this worship the priest must be the elder person of Bhukia family. In "Hareliuansh" the boys are only allowed and it is the planting of a karama branch in the agriculture field. In the month of August-September they celebrate "Nabanna". Each lineage people celebrate "Nabanna" or "Nuakhai" separately.

They can eat new crops during Puja. In the month of September-October they celebrate "Dussehra" and "Garvana Sankranti". In Dussehra they worship Talja Bhabani, Taljakankali and Ashawari. They worship only on Dashami to these deities and sacrifice goats in front of this Goddess. This worship is done by elder member of their family or by Nayak or otherwise called as village headman. In "Garvana Sankranti", mainly married women worships and as a symbol of Laxmi. In the month of October-November they celebrate Diwali, Charu Puja. They celebrate Diwali for two days. On first day they worship Laxmi Devi and on second day they do Gobardhan puja. All these worshiping rituals are done by a married lady. They celebrate Charu Puja for better crops and therefore Banjara people sacrifice goat, cock or any bird at the deities' place. In the month of November-December they celebrate manabasa for the maintenance of peace in the family and for more wealth. In the month of December-January they celebrate Pausa Purnima. In this festival only the unmarried Banjara girls can take part, in which they worship to Jalakamini. In the month of January-February, they celebrate Pedrani Devi Jatara. In the month of February-March, they observe Holi. In the months March-April, they celebrate Sivaratri and Chaitra.

They observe different festivals and worship different deities. Banjara people sacrifice animals in different festivals. In some festivals they also offer coconut, ghee and milk. In the Banjara culture women are strictly restricted from the worship of deities. Only male members can worship. But in two or three cases females are allowed to worship. Banjara people are mainly the devotees of Goddesses. So during the worship of all these Goddesses, to satisfy them Banjara people sacrifice mainly Brown goat, sheep, cock and pigeon etc.

The functionaries who offer worship to deities reside in the village. The functionaries are of three types. The first one is "Nayak" (village head-man), the second category is the Pujari and the third category of ritual functionary is the elder person of the family. All the Banjara people give a great respect to these functionaries.

POLITICAL ORGANISATION

In Banjara society, they have two distinctive types of political organization one is traditional and the other one is modern political organisation. The Banjara call the village council "Milayi" in their language. Five men constitute the quorum of the council; they are village Gountia, Nayak, Village Priest, Dakua and village medicine man. The main task of the milayi is solving village disputes and conducting village festivals. Every decision of the village is made by the Gountia in consultation with other four members of the council and the elder persons of the village. Gountia is the head of the village at inter-village level and intra-village level. Village council solves problems like land disputes family disputes, cases related to misbehavior customary offences, cases of theft etc. Apart from offence trials and settlement of disputes, the council in the meeting fixes the data and other details of the celebration of festival and village rituals. During this period the important aspects of the village are decided by both tradition council and modern political organization i.e. Majhiguda Gram panchayat. The panchayat members and traditional leaders take decisions on behalf of the village Sarpanch Nayak. Sarpanch and the ward members are playing the role of modern leaders of the village.

Villagers, for solving disputes, first take the case to the traditional village council and if the villager feel that the case is beyond its power, then take it to the Majhiguda Gram-panchayat. When the traditional village council and panchayat do not satisfy, then they go to Dharamgad court. Moreover, courts have police power which the council does not have. Hence under compelling circumstance Banjara resort to the court of law.

LIFE CYCLE RITUAL – BIRTH

In the life of human beings, there are various rituals which he or she performs for himself and others, starting from birth to death, which is termed as life cycle rituals.

After marriage pregnancy is very welcomed among Banjaras. A woman's pregnancy indicates rebirth of one of the ancestors. In Banjara culture, a male child is preferred than a female child. Some of the preliminary symptoms of pregnancy include no menstruational monthly cycle, vomiting, spinning of the head and a visible increase in the size of the belly of the woman. After a woman has conceived, she observes several restrictions. The pregnant woman does not have any restrictions in her diet, but they are not allowed to take tamarind, curds and roasted vegetables. After the birth of the child, the mother, the child and the dhai observe the new-born ritual upto seven days in which they are considered impure. They remain in a room, which is called the chutuka for these seven days. They don't worship God, do not touch water or go to the kitchen. They do not take curd or tamarind for these seven days. On the 7thday they wash clothes, clean houses and plaster floor by using cow dung solution. The mother goes to the pond and takes bath with the mixture of turmeric and oil, then she wears new sari and after that, she can touch everybody. Then she is given solution of cow's urine and unboiled milk. She sprinkles all over her and everywhere. She takes baths her hair and child with this solution.

During pregnancy the woman does not go outside the house after evening. They are also not allowed to go anywhere. They wear a Tabij in their hand till the delivery. During the delivery the aged woman remains to oversee the procedure and the delivery is normally done by the dhai.

Puberty: The puberty rites are observed in the same way with certain differences. Inspite of all modernization Banjara people still live as well as maintain their cultural traditions. In Banjara society there is a lot of restrictions for girls. There is no ceremony for boys, when a boy attains maturity. But in case of the girls, the process of maturity becomes quite remarkable because of which with the first coming of menstrual blood; the family members celebrate it. The Banjara knows menstruation as "Handimar". The great aim of initiation is to convert a girl into a fruitful woman. During this puberty stage the Banjara people observe various restrictions.

A girl normally attains maturity at the age of 13 or 14 years. At that time the girl first informs it to her friends, who inform it to the girl's mother. After that, they keep the girl in seclusion for six days in a separate room. If they have no separate room, then they keep the girl at the corner of the house where no male members can see her. At that time, the mother, her sister and all female members of the house take care of the girl. For six days she does not take bath, remains with only worn dress and sits at the corner of the house. Her mother or other female members of the village provide her foods. But she is allowed to wash those utensils. She goes to bath only on the 7th day with other female members of the family, but she does not go alone for bathing. On the seventh day the impure menstrual period is believed to be over. This day is very important for all of them. She washes her hair, massaging turmeric and oil on her body with the help of her sister or other female relatives. After bathing when she comes back to home without turning back and after throwing the unusable dress in water. Then on this day the person who want to make the girl as their daughter-in-law come to girl's house with clothes and other toiletry things. On this day the girl can eat everything but not allow to take non-vegetarian food. The families arrange a feast, in which all the villagers and relatives are invited. The feast does not contain non-vegetarian food. Then they arrange a 'yagyan' to satisfy nine planets, which they call as "Graha-shanti". On this occasion, all the people present gifts to the girl, like ornaments and dress. From that day the girl does not sleep with her mother.

If they do not do this ritual then Banjaras have a belief that, the person who will marry that girl will die soon after the marriage.

Marriage: Marriage is the pivotal social institution in society. It helps satisfy the sexual and bodily needs of human beings in a culturally defined and socially approved way. The Banjara consider marriage as essential for every person of either sex. In Banjara language marriage is called as "Bihaghar". They believe that marriage permits a man and woman to live together as husband and wife and fixes certain rights and duties to bring up the children born of their union.

Among the Banjara clan exogamy is regarded as the basic principle of marriage; but peculiarly enough, subclans (paadas) in most cases are also taken as exogamous groups within a single clan, Banjara can't marry each other because they have a perception that all are brotherand sister to one another. A Banjara man is able to marry more than one woman with general procedure. But a woman once married will not marry again by general procedure.

Cross cousin marriage: Marriage among cousins usually does not take place since marriage in the mother's lineage (khanda) is prohibited. But some times marriages occur with distant cross-cousin which are usually love marriages. Such groom has to give a feast to his kinsman to accept his bride.

But some cases are found in the Hanspada village marrying to near cross cousins. Levirate and sororate are socially sanctioned but never compulsory. But in Banjara society the cases of levirate are not there. But in case of no issue or no male child of the first wife, then the younger sister of the wife is accepted at marriage with prior consent of the wife. After marriage a Banjara sexual relationship is restricted to his/her spouse only. Post-marital sexual relationship with any body other than the spouse is highly punishable and such persons can be out casted from the village. Bride price is not seen in their society.

Marriage at a late age is genetically harmful for them; the boys are married around the age of 20 years and girls get married between 16 to 18 years. But in past days, child marriage was a general practice. Before marriage, permission should be taken from the bride's mother's brother. If bride's mother's brother agrees then the marriage will be arranged, if they are not able to arrange the marriage, it is considered as high position. Arrange marriage is the only system of marriage that is prevalent in their society.

Death Ritual: For Banjara people the concept of death is a very interesting one. They believe in spirits. They have a belief if a person died in middle age or due to any accident then the spirit of that person does not go away. It is always around them and sometimes may cause a lot of harm to them.

Among Banjara when a person dies then all his cousins come to the dead person's house. Then the member of that house eats "Mitti Bhat" which is cooked by other relatives. Then family members and villagers carry the dead body. They keep salt, ghee, rice and cloth toward the north side of the dead body. While taking the dead body they sprinkle coins and shells on the road. Then, they place the dead body at road side when they see a berry plant. After that they take the dead body. The head of the dead body is toward north and the other portion is toward south direction. The elder son gives the funeral pyre, and if the person had no son then any member of his family can give the funeral pyre.

Banjaras call the dead body as "murda". The model in which they carry the dead body is "khat". When they burn the dead body, they do not come back to home until the head of that dead person blasts. The dead body is carried by four persons and the first two persons change their place with the last two persons. Then after coming back from bathing and take the "mitti bhat".

If the dead body needs to be buried in the burial ground or "mashan pada", the length of the hole is 5 ½ to 6m, breadth is 1 inch and depth is 2 feet. But when they dug a big hole for dead body, it also depends on the physical feature of the dead person. If the person is a healthy one then they dig a large hole for him but if he or she is a thin person then they dig a small hole for the dead body.

For each and every type of death they perform different types of rituals;

- If a child has died, then they take it in a pot and dig it behind their houses. They do not take this dead body to burial ground.
- If any Banjara people have died because any diseases like small pox, malaria, chicken pox etc then they do not bury the people. They throw the dead body in to the forest.
- If a married woman has died then Banjara women apply turmeric to the dead body, give a new sari to the dead body, give a bindi which is the mixture of vermilion and sandal etc. then they take the dead body to burial ground. Her elder son gives the funeral pyre. If the woman has no son, then her husband willgive the funeral pyre. Then they take the

remains of body after they are cold, mainly after three days. But in our society, the burnt remains are taken after one day.

When a son dies then the father gives the funeral pyre. If the father dies, then his son carries the dead body. The first two men, carry the dead body are his sons and the last two men who carry the dead body are two brother of the dead man. If the person has no brother, then other member can carry the dead body.

When the funeral pyre is given to the dead body, at that time they give ghee and salt to the dead body so that the ashes do not fly here and there.

Banjara observes this death rituals for ten days. But on eleventh day, they purify themselves.

On 3rd day they clean the house, clothes and wash the house with cow dung water. The washer-man cleans their clothes. The Barber cuts their nail and all members have shaved their heads. But female members only cut their nails. All the family members including other relatives make turban from a cloth for the elder son of the family. The relatives bring the cloth. Then they give a white cloth to the elder son of the family. The cloth is brought by the relatives. Then they give a white cloth to the widow. Then the cousin cooks non-vegetarian food for all members of the house. All members eat that food, except the unmarried girl. The relatives are from another village. In the same village the same clan people are invited for cooking "mittibhat". Then they take the ashes of the dead body in a box and placed it inside the soil above which water pot hangs on a tree and the water drops fall on it. This is done by the male members of the family. The female members light diya in front these ashes both at morning and evening.

This diya is lighted up for ten days. There is no fixed limitation of putting these ashes. They keep these ashes for 5 or 6 years. But when they want or when they have sufficient money they float it in Ganga River. They put the ashes like this so that the bodily remains stay cold in temperature.

After 3 days the Banjara people put water and rice powder in the place where the person died. It occurs at night. Then a symbol is formed on rice powder automatically. Then at that place they put a photograph of the dead person and worship it.

On this day they also invite their "makara", who also bring clothes, sweets and rice with him. Then they cooked it separately for their "makara" and also eat the cooked food within their family. They called it as "maha-prasad". The cousins are invited, they come and cook food then they come back to home. Then they again come on 10th day.

Only from the evening of 3rd day they are semi-purified. They can touch anything from the evening of third day. But before that day they do not touch anything.

On tenth day they eat sweets in the name of the dead person and they believe the soul of the dead person will leave, on the 10th day, from the body remains that are kept inside the soil. On this 10th day they kill goat, sheep and arrange a grand feast for the villagers and cousins with this non-vegetarian foods, sweets, cakes, which are also given to the villagers and to their cousin. They arrange play and "Daskathia" for entertainment, only when the old persons have died.

On the eleventh day they arrange 'yagyan' for the peace

of the soul of dead person. They have a belief that if there is any type of fault in the soul, then by doing yagyan all this will be excused.

The Banjara people call this fault as:

(1) "Ekpa dosha" - One foot.

(2) "Duipa dosha" - Two foot.

During Dussehra they also give "pitrusarat". It is meant for the maintenance at house and peace of the dead ancestors. They invite all the Brahmins. The Brahmins do worship in the name of their dead ancestors. They give curd, honey, fish, rice, potato to Brahmin, which they call as "Dakshina". Then the elder son's wife cooks labsif and puts it into hearth for five times in the name of the dead person and gives five times water into the hearth for washing the hands of their dead ancestors. They have a belief the materials given by them to Brahmins are eaten by their ancestors in heaven. They have a belief the materials given by them to Brahmins are eaten by their ancestors in heaven. They believe, only by doing this, ancestors are satisfied.

These rituals are practiced on these days. They have a belief that only married person's dead body is burnt. But the dead body of unmarried persons is buried in the grave-yard. Some new information has been obtained in the regard. They do not burn all dead bodies. If they get maximum woods then only burn it, otherwise Banjara bury the dead body.

At very early time they burnt the ornaments, and materials with dead body. When an unmarried girl dies, they bury ornaments and the daily dresses of the girl with the dead body. The ladies are not allowed to the graveyard or to perform any burial ritual at the burial ground.

Family: Family is seen all over the world. It is universal from primitive to post modern society. Family is the smallest social unit among Banjara. They believe that through family solidarity, economic cooperation is maintained and the members of family care for the children. Nuclear family is common among them. It includes father, mother and their unmarried children. After marriage everyone goes to live separate because then they can live independently and care for their children in a better way.

Joint family is vanishing day by day in their society. The size of the family varies from 3 to 8 or more members. The head of the Banjara family is generally father. Thus the Banjara family is patrilocal, patrilineal and patriarchal. Polygynous, conjugal family is also seen in their society.

Sexual activity is strictly prohibited within the family or any other consanguine. Banjara are very obliged to elders and show respect towards them; although they live separately and earn independently but all are cooperative with each other and help during difficult situations. In all types of worship all the family members co-operate with each other.

Kinship: Kinship is the organizing principle for social grouping. In Banjara society two types of relationship exist – one is consanguinal and other is affinal. Thus, the Banjara may be called a bilateral group. Kinship terminology plays a vital role in the study of Kinship organisation. Each kinship term refers to status. Without usage of the terms one can't identify the relationship between relaxed friendliness, careful defence, and the obligation to co-operate. Banjara use both classificatory and descriptive terminology socially.

The tribe has six main clans and each clan had several subclans (padas). But we have found only four main clans in our base-village. Marriage is strictly prohibited within their sub-clans members. In their respective clan there is a Kinship network. There is no system of political bargaining or pressure group formation for the interest of the clan members. The clan members of the same generation regard each other as brothers and sisters. In marriage ceremony, death rituals and name giving ceremony, the consanguinal and affinal Kin members have some particular role and rights for maintenance of the rituals. The Kinship system in essence is a network of social relations of dyadic type. In its network the rights and duties of relatives to one another is redefined by social usage. Kinship usage, as universal phenomenon of each and every culture, are also perceive among the Banjaras. Among the Banjara (in more or less degree) the Kinship usage like joking, avoidance, respect, teknonymy and restraint are observed. All these usages are seen between their family members.

Succession and Inheritance: Among the Banjara, succession and inheritance of name, clan name, property, residence, office, headmanship. Priestship, etc are patrilineal. Generally, the males are the owner of the land and other wealth. After the death of parents, the total wealth is inherited to their sons in Banjara society. The sons equally distribute their lands. If the daughter wants to get parental wealth, she can take the wealth. In case of ornaments the parents give them as their legal wealth. In case of no male child issue an adopted son inherits the property and all. An adopted son-in-law inherits the property in case of no male child. In case of only female child issue, an adopted son-in-law inherits the property in his name.

Relationship with Neighbours: The Banjara of Dabriguda and Hanspada villages are co-operative and friendly with each other. They make friendship very soon with the other castes, tribes and outsiders. They keep peace and good relationship with their neighbour. Most of Banjaras establish various ceremonial and artificial relationships with their neighbouring castes, tribes, and address one another with end earing name. They actively participate in the marriage ceremonies, birth and death rituals and always stand behind anyone who needs help in any regard. They have enough faith on their neighbours. The neighbours look after the little children when both the parents are out of home to earn their livelihood.

EDUCATION

In the village Dabriguda, there is only one primary school and no high school. There is one high school at Majhiguda. The student of Dabriguda village goes to Majhiguda high school for getting their further education. In Hanspada there is one primary school. In primary school, the students of Banjara tribe are given mid-day meal and education equipments like chalk, slates, pencil, books by D. P.E.P. center of Koksara block. There is a college each about 5 and 7 kms away from Dubriguda and Hanspada respectively. The Banjara people are interested to provide more education to boys than girls. But now a day they send their girls to school for better education. The main reason is to marry their daughter to a service holder. Where as the boys are required to pursue studies and higher studies because of service, knowledge and to get a high status in society. Through D.P.E.P. center each primary school got Rs 2000 per year for minor repairing. The primary school provides dress to the students who are living in below poverty line and attend the class regularly.

The lists indicate that the following number of educational institutions are under Koksara block:

1.	Number of Primary School	-----	101
2.	Number of M.E. School	-----	09
3.	Number of College	-----	02
4.	Number of High School	-----	17
5.	Number of Girls High School	-----	01
6.	Number of V.G.M.E.S.	-----	14

LANGUAGE

The Banjara people in Kalahandi district are speaking a language, which is mixture of Hindi and Chattisgadi. But now due to influence of local Kalahandi language some of them speak in Oriya. They speak in Hindi and some of them also know English for writing purpose.

LEISURE, TIME AND RECREATION

The Banjara have a lot of leisure time because most of the villagers are dependent on agriculture. During the lean period when they don't go to the fields, they resort to daily wage labour. The females also go to the fields during harvesting period. Whenever they get leisure time, the Banjara watch television and listen to radio. The young boys play different types of games like cricket, basket ball etc. Some women make emboidery work on their dress, sari too. The females take care of the houses and keep it neat and clean. They also look after their children in many cases. They also assist to male members in the worshipping of different types of deities. Some Banjara people are sometimes busy in smoking bidi, hooka and drinking tea. In rainy season Banjara people do not go outside, so most of them spend their time with their family members.

FOOD, NUTRITION AND HEALTH

Food is one of the basic need of life, nutrition is essential for maintenance of good health. Due to the economical status of the people the richer families can afford to purchase different edible food from the market but the poor group can't afford. Generally, the Banjara people can eat only two times a day but youngsters take foods three times in a day. On the morning they take red tea and salt. Rice is the principal food which is usually taken by the rich families. But the poor families take mandia powder. Those who are daily wage labourers, they take Harida powder during the lean seasons. They also take rice or Mandia, watered rice, Chili and dry fish. Women do not take good food due to the scarcity of food in winter season. Women member do not eat chicken or mutton as they worship to Laxmi Devi. They collect several fruits, roots, flower, and leaves from the forests. In most of the traditional diets the quality of diet has changed due to deforestation. Most of the traditional diets are not available. During the lean season when there is acute food scarcity, they also take Badi and other dried vegetables and fruits. No special food is given during pregnancy period of Banjara woman. After confinement they give a juice of jaggery, ghee, garlic and sunthi. They called it as 'Kad'. For child they boil wheat and mixed with ghee, sugar called as lapsib. In summer season they drink palua pani to make end meet. Poverty, the problem of malnutrition and under nutrition are found in great extents. The problem of under nourishment is causing serious concern due to its manifestation in the form of vitamin 'A' deficiency, anemia, Goiter, due to these children are suffering from night blindness, anemia and several other nutrional deficiency diseases. No marked improvement has been noticed in the nutritional status particularly of women and children.

Banjara believed that a person is healthy when he is not suffered from any disease and has to perform all the hard physical labour. The symptom of fever in the Banjara society is weakness, staying all day in bed and not able to do daily work. The concept of illness in the Banjara society is that when a person colour changed to pale, unable to work and suffering from itching in body. The younger people considered to be healthy because they can work hard and usually free from disease. The Banjara are mainly suffering from several disease syphilis, Gonorrhea and hernia etc.

They strongly believe that some diseases are due to supernatural spirits and other malevolent beings. At first they try to find the cure with the help of shaman, who gives them traditional and indigenous system of medicines then they go to hospital at last stage when they do not recover after usage of traditional medicines.

DRESS AND ORNAMENTS

Earlier the Banjara people wear hand stitched clothes. But now they wear dresses purchased from the local market. The Banjara female members wear Ghagra called as "phetua" and Blouse called as "kacheli". But now the female members wear sari as their dress pattern in a North Indian style.

Mirror, Kaudi, Adiaa of silver, Jhulpi of silver are attached to their traditional dress Ghagar. These dresses are stitched upwith different colored cloths from different yarns.

The male members wear dhoti. It is 1.5m piece of cloth, stitched up with different colours of wool, with mirror and silver finish in the borders. But now they wear lungi, coloured shirts, and pants. The Banjara children wear half shirts, pants, scouts, salwar and sometimes the young girls wear sari. Male members use Turbans or "pagadi". But now a day they use it occasionally. They called Gamucha as 'sapi', and Kurta or shirt as "Jhagala"

The Banjara women love ornaments. They adorn different types and designs of ornaments to decorate their body. They use hansli, mala, panri, kanthi, pagadi, kandor, sonanath, soralurki, bauli, baunta, guna, kakni and banori, chudi, poenchi, eetti, topli and ghugri, anthi, echua etc. During marriage functions, they use chuda which is of silver. But now a day they use Lurki, guna, Kanthi, Chudi, Pagdi, echua.

	Ornaments	**Their Usage**
1.	Hansli	neck, made of silver
2.	Mala	neck (silver)
3.	Panri	leg (silver)
4.	Kanthi	neck (gold)
5.	Pagadi	leg (silver payal)
6.	Kandor	waist (silver)
7.	Sono Nathin	nose to ear (gold)
8.	Soro	lurkiear (gold)
9.	Baulitop	earring (silver)
10.	Baunta	upper arm (silver)
11.	Guna	Both side of nose (gold)
12.	Kakni & Banori	Bangle arms (silver)
13.	Chudi	Bangles (glass)

14.	Paenchi	both arms (silver)
15.	Eetti	Ring of coin, worn in right hand, 4th and 3rd finger.
16.	Topli and ghugri	Top of forehead. Topli in both side of head in the middle of head (silver)
17.	Anthi	Put on khosha (wool)
18.	Echua	on the toes, 2nd and 3rd toes (silver)
19.	Lurki	Gold earring

On Marriage: The dress pattern and other requirements of Banjara are given below:

1.	Pagadi	Turban on head (Red colour)
2.	Jhugala	Kurta
3.	Pachedato	to cover body, like shawl
4.	Shela	2 in number, put on shower
5.	Tangaru	Thread (both ear red colour)
6.	Deti	used to keep katari
7.	Talwar	used for fighting holds in right hand
8.	Dhaal	holds in left hand

INTER-ETHNIC INTERACTION

In the Banjara village there are eight caste groups. They are Brahmin, Karana, Gaud, Banjara, Halwa, Sunda, Gond, Barik and Dom. Earlier each cast of the group depended mainly on traditional occupations. Brahmin, the most dominant group of village depended on priest-hood and agriculture, Karana on agriculture, Gauda on animal husbandry and supplying milk, Banjara on business, Halwa on agriculture, Sundi on liquor making, Gond on agriculture

Barik on hair cutting and shaving and Dom on weaving cloths and preparing leather shoes. Thus each caste group of the village has its own traditional occupation. But now the whole economic structure has undergone change by coming into contact with urban centers. Interaction always occurs between these caste groups. But they always continue to maintain some restriction between them.

The Banjara can go and sit in the courtyard of Brahmin, Karana and Gauda. In case of dry food, the Banjara people can take vegetables from all castes. Banjaras take oil from all caste members. In case of dining, Banjaras can only dine with their own caste members. But in case of accepting water Banjara people can take water from Brahmin, Karana and Gauda.

But now-a-days due to impact of urbanization all these restrictions among different castes are lessening slowly.

3

GODS AND SPIRITS

> "God is idealized and compared to father, it can be said that the conception of deities vary with different places like the father has in the family in different types of society".
>
> *(Freud in E.E.Evans-pritchard: 1965, 10)*

Religion may be described as a system of beliefs and practices directed toward the "ultimate concern" of a society. 'Ultimate concern' concept has two aspects – meaning and power. It has meaning in the sense of ultimate meaning of central values of a society, and it has power in the sense of ultimate, sacred, or supernatural power, which stand behind those values. The religion of all primitive societies mainly consists of beliefs and practices, where beliefs are mainly theory and worship is the practice. (W.A. Lessa, 1958:1)

CONCEPT OF GODS AND SPIRITS

From time immemorial the development of human beings along with the civilization though chronologically upgraded due to the power of brain of a human being but he is not the sole father as claimed. Besides, various scholars believed that supernatural powers always act upon the creation. Religion rests on beliefs and beliefs rest on the supernatural being. According to Wilhelm Schmidt, "Everything develops from simpler and cruder. He thought there is a stage 'Mana' before animism in which the idea of lucky, the canny and uncanny, is the sole constituent of what he called supernatural". Andrew Lang said, "Supreme being of primitive people is at any rate in many cases, not spirit at all, at least in our sense of divine spirit. God is spirit and those who worship him must worship him in spirit and in truth. Supernatural being is mainly classified in two forms, one is of non-human origin and other is human origin. Those of non-human origin are Gods or deities and those of human origin are ghosts and ancestral spirits. Both the forms are represented in anthro-pomorphic forms.

The former category of supernatural entities is known as Gods or Goddesses whereas the latter is known as spirits (Oliver, 1981:3911).

Gods

According to mythology the beliefs, myths, dogmas, and legends were the creator of the Gods, not merely a means of winning their favor. God represents the subjective pole and it claims to possess the highest meaning and value in the total experience. God is very closely associated with the word 'Religion' which is only found in human society. The God of Religion is concrete and determinate. If we look at the logical argument made by Kant, God is the sum of all positive attributes and existence. In any positive attribute or positive meaning affirmative of existence, God exists. Howells divides God as creator Gods, culture bringers, departmental deities. A creator God is one who created the world and everything in it. A culture bringer God is one who is responsible for introducing crucial elements of culture.

This god first gave the idea of states and agriculture. A departmental deity is one, who is in charge of a specific area of activity such as weather. Belief in a single God is monotheism and belief in many Gods is polytheism. So it is said by various philosophers that God is omnipresent, omnipotent and omniscient. His power of omnipotent is reflected in various supernatural entities. Faiths in these super natural entities bring various customs and traditions in the society which in latter form is defined as religion (Oliver, 1981:353-35).

Deities

According to Freud, God is idealized and compared to father, it can be said that the conception of deities vary with the very different places of the father has in the family in different types of society.

Spirits

Sprits are less remote than God and a good deal, more approachable.These are always near to us. According to Maxmuller, after death of man the body becomes soul. The soul then becomes spirit which is very important, which may be malevolent and benevolent. This malevolent and benevolent power connects to ancestral deity. Tylor also said dreams give birth to soul for existence of spirit and in later stage of culture become that of God. So the world of spirit is the mental world. Spirit is an immaterial symbol of 'Mana'. It makes easier to adjust to our environment because they humanize it. Spirits are either deites, who never materialize or ghost i.e. soul of the dead. The most common form of worship is intimate conversation with a spirit, which is believed by most of the tribal people.

DIFFERENT TYPES OF GODS AND GODDESSES

The Banjara people are mainly devotees of goddess. They are very much restricted to their culture. They are much more influenced by Orissa culture and Hindu beliefs and practices due to their inhabitant. The Banjaras are having

Supernatural Beings

REMOTE | NON-REMOTE

REMOTE:

SKY	UNDER GROUND
1. Dharam Devata (M)	1. Charukhuta(F)
2.Chand Devata (M)	

NON-REMOTE:

CLAN/ LINEAGE	HILL AND FOREST	WATER AND LAND	VILLAGE
1.Taljakankali(F)	1.Jalakamini(F)	1.Jalakamini(F)	1.Danteswari(F)
2.Dula(M)	2.Swarga Maili(F)	2.Mati Devi(F)	2.Mati Devi(F)
3.Pedrani(F)		3.Mera Maa(F)	3.Banjari(F)
4.Taljabhabani(F)			4.Phulamauli(F)
5.Meramaa(F)			5.Mera Maa(F)
6.Ashawari(F)			6.Matrala(F)
7.Ancestral Sprit (ishana devata)			7.Lukudia(M)
			8.Basterein(F)
			9.Thakurani(F)
			10.Barsarmajhi(M)
			11.Daragadhiani(F)
			12.Bhandarshuni(F)
			13.Badamaili(F)
			14.Sanamaili(F)
			15.Holikadevi(F)

a peculiar concept about Gods and Goddesses. They believe Lord Siva as God or Bhagabana and Devi as Thakura. They called Brahma, Vishnu and Maheswara are called as God (Bhagabana). But called others as Thakura.

Non-Remote Deities

A. Hill and Forest Deities

A.1) Banjari Devi: Banjari Devi is one deity among many forest deities.The name of Banjari Devi is given by Banjara according to their own culture. Whenever the Banjara migrate from one place to another, they establish a Banjari Devi in the new place. Ladies are not allowed to be present during the worship. Banjari Devi is worshipped during Dussehra and also during marriage, when the bridegroom is ready to go the bride's house. This worship is done outside the village under "kendu" tree during Dussehra (Dashami). It is mainly done by the village headman, whom they call as 'Nayak'. He is the main priest.

At first they worship only a red cloth tied around small wooden parts. But now they worship a lady sitting on bull, who they think as Banjari Devi. She is very aggressive in nature. When it occurs they sacrifice a brown goat (Khairea Bakra) for pacification and satisfaction of the goddess.

Banjara people worship her to avoid unfortunate events and succeed in various fields. The Banjara people think all Devis are very much aggressive in nature and the way to satisfy them is by sacrificing.

A.2) Swarga Maili- There is a small hill at the end of the village which the Banjara people worship. This worship is done collectively by 7 to 8 villages, namely Mahima,

Temera, Majhiguda, Hanspada, Khursali, pada, Mundapada and Dabriguda asking for rain. It is done in the month of July-August on Tuesday. For rain they worship Swarga Maili Devi who is placed on the Hill top.

They worship to the footprint of Goddess. She is not very aggressive in nature. In spite of that they sacrifice black cock, black male goat (kalia bakra), white pigeon (male) etc. The foot print is five feet away from a well, which is now filled with sand. But when they worship the Devi, it rains and the well is filled with water. This well is covered by something which they call as "Dunguri".

Male member who is of Temera village does this worship. Females are not allowed to attend this worship. The priest must be a married one and the person who goes there must also be married.

B. Water and Land Deities

B.1) Jalakamini: The Banjara people celebrate New Year. They called it as "pausa purnima". It occurs in the end of December or first of January on Thursday. On this day they worship Jalakamini. Mainly unmarried girls go for bathing in morning. They take jaggery (gol) with them. Then they mix it with water in a pot and then offer in the name of Jalakamini. They think the goddess Jalakamini resides in water. She is not very aggressive in nature; therefore, no sacrifice is offered. Male members are not allowed. It is done by female members.

B.2) Mati Devi: Literally 'Mati' means soil. This deity is called the deity of soil. The Mati Devi is placed in a room at the village end. This is called "Matighara" into which ladies are not allowed. It is a hewnstone, which is kept facing towards west, when the priest's face is towards east. She is less aggressive in nature, therefore sacrifices are given not in every occasion. She is worshiped during Dussehra and on every Tuesday. Ladies are not allowed even if to eat its sacred offal. It is done mainly for welfare of village and villagers. She is under 'Neam', 'Jashibala' and 'Khajuri' tree.

B.3) Meramaa: Meramaa is another important Goddess propitiated by Banjara people. During Tij festivals the girls mainly spread sand in the name of Meramaa, whom they worship. This worship is performed within the village, in an open place of village. The face of Devi is kept towards East. Meramaa is worshipped on every Tuesday or Saturday.

Meramaa is not very aggressive in nature. Inspite of that black goat is sacrificed. The priest by whom this worship is performed must be an unmarried one and he should be a member of Rathod family. Male members can take part. This is done mainly for the protection of cows and bulls. The cows and bulls are free of all diseases. Female members can't take its sacred offal. She is under 'Neam tree'.

So Banjara people are not so much primitive in nature. But they are very conservative in nature. In their society there is a lot of restriction for women which we can know by seeing their different types of worship. They feel women are ritually impure as they pass through menstruation every month. That's why, during many of their worshipping, women are allowed only to arrange the worship but barred from taking part or consumption of the offals presented in front of the deities.

The Banjara also worship their natural land marks like hill, forest, water and land. Each one represents a specific deity with some power. In all these rituals only males are allowed to take part. Females are not allowed to take part in this worship or to take sacred offals. Only in few of the worship, they can take part and take sacred offerals. Mud and Jharabala clan people worship Meramaa.

C. Village Gods and Goddesses

C.1) Danteswari: Among all the village deity Danteswari is their main village Goddess. She is identified as a cement tomb which they called as 'Bhat' in the middle of village in an open place. Infront of Danteswari, a male deity named Lukudia is present, who helps Danteswari in her work.

She is not so aggressive in nature and is worshipped for good luck and success in any work. Banjara people have great faith on Danteswari. She is worshipped during Dussehra on Dashami. Her face is towards the east direction of village. In Behera village there is a great temple of Danteswari.

As Goddess, Danteswari is worshipped in village level. So women are strictly restricted to participate and take its sacred offal. But they can only witness the ritual from a distance.

C.2) Phula Mauli: Phula Mauli is another Goddess of Banjara, who is worshipped in the agricultural land. She is very much aggressive in nature therefore sacrifices are given. This worship is done only for increasing the fertility of land, so that they can get more amount of rice. This worship is done on Tuesday in the month of March-April. It is nothing but a basket with flowers on the land is worshipped. Females are not allowed to go there.

Case Study: A person named Ghanasyama Naik (age-31) he tried to build a dam on their so-called "Sagar" but did not get success. A pregnant woman died in that particular water. The spirit of that pregnant woman came in the dream of Ghanasyama, and told him to worship in the name of 'Phulamauli Devi'.

The Dabriguda village people believe that only Gountia' family people can catch fish from this 'Sagar'. Before fishing the 'Gountia' people worship on the sand in the name of 'Phulamauli' by which they can succeed in fishing.

C.3) Matrala: Matrala is also another God of Banjara people. There is no specific ritual for this worship. It is a hewn stone facing towards east. It is present under the tree. The Banjara worship mainly in the month of August on Saturday.

She is very aggressive in nature. Therefore, they sacrifice brown goat (khairea Bakra). This worship is performed by 'Nayak' (the village man) at the village end. Only male members are allowed to take part in this Puja.

The Banjara people during ancient times worshipped this hewn stone. But now there is nothing under the tree and there is also no restriction about which type of tree. Besides that, they worship under the tree the name of Matrala. This worship is done mainly for protection of cow, bull and cattle. By doing this Puja they are not affected by any disease. Females are strictly restricted to go there and eat sacred offal. Oriya people of this village called this deity as 'pardeshni'. They worship her during Chittalagi Amabasya, Dussehra, Chaitra purnima etc.

C.4) Lukudia- The God Lukudia is placed infront of Danteswari. It is in form of a 'Bhat' (a pillar of cement). He is not very aggressive in nature. Therefore, only by sacrificing a black cock, he can be satisfied. He is worshipped with Danteswari by village chief (Nayak) in the month of October during Dussehra. He is in the middle of village facing towards west and also towards Danteswari. His work is only to help Danteswari in her work. Females are allowed to see puja but can't take its sacred offal.

C.5) Basterein: It is a village level worshipping. This worship occurs at the village end. It has a temple of its own and the face of the Goddess is towards east. She is not very aggressive in nature and only yellow colour flower pleases her.

She is worshiped by village priest (mainly of Gond tribe or of Ghasi caste) during Chaitra Amabasya, Dussehra and Chittalagi Amabasya. They sacrifice a black pigeon and brown goat infront of her. Because they think by sacrificing animal, the Devi will give them more wealth and they can maintain a prosperous life. She is also worshipped for the creation of abundant rain.

C.6) Thakurani: The place where a hewn stone is placed is called as "Devir Asana" and that house or room is called as "Devata Ghar". That stone is called as "Thakurani Gudi", she is another Banjara goddess placed at the village end in a separate house made up of mud and bamboo, facing towards west.

She is very much aggressive in nature therefore black male goat and pumpkin are sacrificed infront of her. She is very much influential by her work. Anger of the deity causes chicken pox, small pox etc. People worship her in the month of July (every Tuesday) besides this they also worship her in Dussehra and Chittalagi Amabasya. She is worshipped for freedom from diseases and also for abundant rain.

C.7) **Barsarmajhi:** Barsarmajhi is the male deity of Banjara people. He was the priest of Basterein. But after his death, to give a respect to him they keep a stone in the name of Barsarmajhi at the door of Basterein Devi and worship him. He is placed along with Basterein at the outside of village facing towards west direction.

He is not very much aggressive in nature. He is worshiped by village priest in Chittalagi Amabasya, Chaitra and Dussehra. They sacrifice black male goats or sheep in front of him. He is worshipped mainly to defeat enemies in war and for sufficient rain. Women are strictly restricted to witness the Puja.

Banjara people worship these three deities namely Basterein, Thakurani, Barsarmajhi mainly for rain and also sacrifice animals in their names. The ritual practices during this worship are described in the next chapter.

C. 8) Daragadhiari: Daragadhiari is the female deity of Banjara people. The Banjara people worship her at village level. She is worshipped at village end under the "Neam tree" and "Gud tree" in form of a hewnstone and marked by vermilion.

She is not very aggressive in nature. Banjara people sacrifice male black goats infront of her. This worship is performed by village priest on every Tuesday during Dussehra, Chittalagi Amabasya.Women are not allowed to witness the puja and take its sacred offal. She is mainly worshipped for welfare of the village and villagers. Banjaras said to me that by doing this worship, they are leading a normal and peaceful life.

C .9) Bhandarshuni: Bhandarshuni is another Banjara female deity. She is worshipped at village end under a palm tree, in the form of new stone. She is not very much aggressive in nature. She is worshipped by village priest (mainly of S.C. group), outside the village and a black sheep is sacrificed infront of her. Bhandarshuni is worshipped during Dussehra, Chittalagi Amabasya etc. Women are restricted to go during this ceremony. They worship Bhandarshuni for welfare of village people.

C.10) Bada Maili and Sana Maili: Both of these deities are worshipped by Banjara at the end of the village at the same time.

They are not aggressive in nature. They are two sisters. Badamaili is under the 'Neam', 'Palsa' and 'Papir' tree and Sanamaili is under the palm tree, habiscus and 'simuli' tree. Village priest worships both of them and it is a hewn stone in front of which black sheep are sacrificed for Badamili and Sanamaili. They think this idol as the Badamaili and another for Sanamaili. They are worshipped during Dussehra (Dashami), Chittalagi Amabasya and every Tuesday. Women are restricted to go there.

So the worship of Bhandarshuni, Daragadhiani, Badamaili and Sanamaili occur on the same occasion one after another. So in the village level worshipping, they first put a vermilion mark to deity and always sacrifice animals. Usually ladies are strictly restricted to witness the worship even if they are not allowed to take the sacred offal.

Besides all these village deities they (Banjara) worship another Goddess, Kali Devi, she is very well known to us and also famous in Hindu society.

Kali Devi: Kali Devi is not purely a Banjara deity. There is an idol of Maa Kalika in a house, which is outside the village, or at the village end with the Thakurani Devi.

She is very much aggressive in nature. She is worshipped by a Brahmin priest. Only old male Banjaras are allowed to worship her. This worship occurs during Dussehra. They bring the priest from another village. The Banjara people sacrifice black cock and pigeon etc. The face of Devi is towards east.

Banjara people occasionally invited the Brahmin priest to perform worship, because Brahamins never sacrifice any animal in front of the Devi. Most of the Banjara Gods and Goddess want scarifices. Therefore, Brahmin priest can only do the 'deva' puja. That's why in every occasion they call their own priest who is acquainted with all their rituals.

Family or Clan Deities

The Banjara people worship different deities at family level; different clan people worship different deities.There are eight clans, with different 'Esta Devi or Devata'. These are given below:

1. Taljakankali: Taljakankali is the most influential goddess of Banjara. She is placed inside the house called as "Devataghar" facing towards east. The priest (Nayak) who worshipped her faces towards west.

The goddess is in form of an idol of gold over which an umbrella is placed. She is very much aggressive in nature.

She is worshipped during Dussehra (October). They worship Talja Kankali to defeat their enemy and for family welfare. Ladies are not allowed to witness the worship but they can take the sacred offal. The Banjara people sacrifice male black goat in front of her. Taljakankali is worshipped along with Taljabhabani. She is the 'Ista Devi' of Laudia and Pamar clan members.

2. **Taljabhabani:** Goddess Taljabhabani is placed in the 'Devataghar' facing towards east. Village chief (Nayak) worships her. Taljabhabani is an idol of bronze and is placed with Taljakankali. She is also very much aggressive in nature. She is also worshipped during Dussehra. They worship her to defeat enemy and also for family welfare. The 'Nayak' sacrifices brown goat in front of her. Ladies are allowed o take sacred offal but can't witness worship. When she gets annoyed then chicken pox and measles break out among people or that's what the Banjaras believe to this day.

Taljabhabani is the 'Ista Devi' of Bhukia, Ortia and Kelut clan members. So the rituals practiced during these two deities are same because both of them are worshipped at same time.

3. **Dula:** Dula is another male deity of Banjara people. This worship is done during Dussehra and every Saturday. It is in the form of a hewn stone.

He is aggressive in nature. A male black sheep is sacrificed in front of him. People worship him for family welfare. Elder person of their family worships Dula. The face of the God is towards East. There is no such marked ritual at the time of worshipping of Dula.

He is the 'Ista Deva' of Banat clan people.

4. Pedrani: Pedrani Devi is another powerful Goddess of Banjara. She is also named as 'Durputa' or 'Gopabali' or 'Koman' Devi.

They worship Pedrani Devi in form of an idol of stone. She is very aggressive in nature. She is worshipped in 'Devataghar' facing towards west. They worship her for fulfillment of individual wishes. She is worshipped in every 15 days (mainly on Sunday). In the 'Maghapanchami' (Jan-Feb) the Banjara people do Pedrani Jatara, in which all people participate.

Mainly the Bhukia clan people worship Pedrani and she is their 'Ista Devi'. Anger of the deity causes diarhhea, stomach ache etc. At first Pedrani Devi was not their deity. But after some unfortunate events they started to worship Pedrani Devi.

Case Study

Kalabati (29years) told me that a lady from Madhya Pradesh brought with her many gold ornaments in dowry and with these ornaments, a goddess named Durputa or Pedrani Devi. All the family members of that lady (her name is Srimati) suffered from various diseases like dysentery, fever, and stomach ache. Though they had an idea of what might be causing the diseases, they didn't do any rituals infront of any deity. Kalabati also suffered from the disease and lost a lot of strength but was some how strong enough to keep going. Upon the villagers' consultance with the village priest, he said that if that disease wasn't cured, may be it was the wrath of Pedrani Devi, and if it would be cured soon then it might be the wrath of some other deity. But the disease started spreading like wild fire. The goddess came in Kalabati's dreams and told her that because she had a child of her own, she had prestige in the society and therefore the goddess came to reside inside her ordering everyone else to worship Pedrani Devi. Then they started worshipping of Pedrani Devi.

Then all the members of that village also suffered from these diseases. After that Devi came in the dream of everyone and said to worship her. The entire village started to worship her due to this incident.

Informant: Chandrabhanu (31years)was also first unaware about the power of Durputa Maa. He did not worship her. Then Maa came to his dreams and advised him to worship her. After worshipping Maa, Chandrabhanu and other members were cured from disease. They led a peaceful life.

5. Ashawari: Ashawari is another goddess of Banjara people. But she is worshipped mainly in the 'Nayak' family of Keluta clan. They worship a Talwar and Dhaal as a symbol of Ashawari Devi. She is not very aggressive in nature. The 'Talwar Dhaal' is also placed in the 'Devta ghar'. This worship occurs during Dussehra.This worship occurs mainly for defence purpose. They sacrifice a male black goat. Ladies are allowed to take sacred offals but can't witness the Puja.

There is no specific ritual for this worship. Besides all these deities, Banjara people also worship Laxmi, Trinatha, Brundabati and Dhalangar, which are described below.

Laxmi Devi: Laxmi Devi is worshipped inside the house, facing towards east.

Mainly married ladies worship her on every Thursday and also on 'Sudashabrata'. She is not very much aggressive in nature. Most of the people worship the photo of Laxmi

Devi. They worship Laxmi Devi for more wealth and to maintain peace in the house. She does not need any sacrifice.

Trinatha Mela: In this worship Banjara people worship three Gods namely Brahma, Vishnu and Maheswar.

It is done by Brahmin priest inside the house facing towards west. The Banjara people take three betel leaves in the name of Brahma, Vishnu and Maheswar and put a nut above it and worship it. This worship occurs on Sunday (evening). These deities are not aggressive in nature and females are allowed to watch the puja. They worship him for begetting male off springs and for maintaining of peace in the house. There is not any marked ritual. No sacrifice is given.

Brundabati:- Brundabati in their female deity, mainly married women can worship her and put water to the 'Tulsi plant' to whom they called as Brundabati.

She is not very much aggressive in nature and is placed in front of house facing towards west. She is worshipped regularly in the month of October and November specially. She is worshipped for the welfare of family members and for appeasement of soul.

Many people of Ghatikia placed the idol Parvati goddess and Sandhyabati along with the Tulsi plant and worshipped. The male members can worship but the person may be a married one and also take 'Karnamantra' from any 'Guru'. The above mentioned deities don't need any kind of animal or fruit sacrifices.

Dhalangar: Dhalangar Devi is placed in the 'Devata ghar' of Banjara people. She has no idol at all. She is not aggressive in nature. She is worshipped on every Tuesday along with other clan level deities.

They sacrifice a black goat in front of her and she is worshipped by male members and the elders of family. By taking the sacred offals of Dhalangar, a barren lady bears child. This belief was prevalent in ancient times but now they do not have such types of feeling.

So females are allowed to take sacred offals of this Devi but can't witness the puja. There is not any specific ritual for her.

Pir: Pir is the male deity and is placed in 'Devata ghar' facing towards east. He is worshipped only on Diwali. He is not very aggressive in nature. He is worshipped only for family welfare and mainly sweets are given to him as sacred offerings. Ladies are allowed to take sacred offals.

So in the worshipping of all the family level deities female are allowed to take the sacred offals but can't take part in it.

In this table list below, a chart of all clan and their Istadevi/deva is given.The clan people whose Istadevi is Taljakankali, they also worship Taljabhabani with her. The Kelut clan people whose Ista devi is Talja Bhabani is also worshiped Ashawari mainly at the time of worshipping of Taljabhabani etc.

Name of clan	Ista Devi or Deva
Laudia and Pamar	Talja Kankali
Bhukia, ortia and Kelut	Talja bhabani
Banat	Dula
Bhukia	Pedrarior Durpata maa
Kelut	Ashawari
Mud and Jharabala	Mera Maa

Another list is given below–

Trees under which the Deity is found	Name of the Goddess
Neam and Gud	Daragadhiani
Palm	Bhandarshuni
Neam, Palsa, Papir	Badamaili
Palm, hibiscus, simuli	Sana maili
Neam	Meramaa
Neam, Jashimala, Khajuri	Mati Devi

Remote Deities

A. Underground

Charukhuta: Remote deities are those who are mainly away form their living place. Charukhuta is one of them, to whom Banjara people worship under soil.

Charukhuta is the female deity and Banjara worship her in agricultural land. They only worship the soil in the name of Charukhuta.The face of the Goddess is towards east.

She is not very aggressive in nature. Ladies are strictly restricted to witness the puja and take the sacred offal. They worship Charukhuta for better quality and quantity of crops.

B. Sky

B.1 Dharam Devata: The Banjara people worship to Dharam Devata in the sky. In our sense the Dharam Devata is Sun God.

He is not aggressive in nature. No sacrifices are given to him on Diwali, Dussehra and Kartika Purnima. The people (mainly married male person) go for bath to the pond (their term – munda). Then they offer water in the name of

Dharam Devata in pond and light agarbati to him. The face of the person while worshipping to Sun is towards face of the God which is towards west.

B. 2 Chand Devata: Chand is another God of Banjara. All the villagers worship him in the month of pausa. He is the sky God. He is not aggressive in nature and therefore sacrifices are not given and also there is not any restriction in his worship.

This is all about Banjara deities which they classify in a peculiar way. But I have marked one thing, that the people's idea of deity. They think mainly the Goddess are aggressive in nature therefore sacrifices are given and restriction are maintained. But Gods are not aggressive in nature, therefore no sacrifices are given.

Name of the Deities	Sacrifices
Banjari Devi	Brown goat (m)
Swargamaili	Black goat, white pigeon (m)
Mati Devi	Pig, Brown goat (m)
Meramaa	Black goat (m)
Danteswari	Brown goat and cock (m)
Phulamauli	Big male goat
Matrala	Brown goat (m)
Lakudia	Black cock
Basterein	Black pigeon and Brown goat (m)
Thakurani	Black goat (m) and a pumpkin
Barsarmajhi	Black goat and Sheep (m)
Daragadhiani	Black goat (m)
Bhandharshuni	Black Sheep
Bada and Sanamaili	Pigeon and Black cock

Kali Devi	Pigeon and Black cock
Aljakankali	Black goat (m)
Talja bhabani	Black goat (m)
Dula	Black Sheep
Pedrani	Lemon and Black goat
Ashawari	Black goat (m)
Dhalangar	Black goat (m)
Pir	Sweets

The Banjara people also worship 'Isana Devata'. But the various ritual activities practices in this worship are given in the next chapter.

Sprit: The world of supernatural beings of Banjara people consist of both benevolent (Good) and malevolent (Bad) sprits. There are some specialists or experts who act as the medium between the Banjara people and spirits. The people in most of the cases go to the 'Gunia'. There is no definite way or special types of ancestral spirits. The head of the family perpetuates that the ancestral spirits are present in many occasions of festivals. Sprits are unlike ghosts. They do not cause various troubles to people after that death.

Case Study

Informant: Syamlal Nayak's elder brother. The elder brother told that Syamlal had committed suicide. His soul entered into various other people of his village and caused a great harm to them. Then the affected people went to their sorcerer (gunia). The sorcerer read *mantras* and offered various foods which Syamlal liked very much. After that he went away from the body of those people and the people resumed their normal life.

A.4. Thengua a ghost: When a young unmarried boy dies, his ghost becomes more powerful. He can enter the body of anyone. The Banjara people believe that if the spirit has affair with any girl or if any girl of that village has sexual relation with any other boy, in that case the spirit enters into the body of such unmarried girl. When sorcerer reads sacred spell then the spiritis automatically controlled by him. The spirit is more powerful in Amabasya and full Moon day.

A.5. Chirangul: When a pregnant woman dies then the spirit is called as Chirangul by Banjara. When it enters into body then it is very dangerous and does harm too many people. Banjara people believe when they hear a sound of crying from a distance then they say it is the Chirangul. But it is controlled by sorcerer. In case the pregnant woman died after the birth of her child, then the Chirangul does not affect her child.

A.6 The person who died by God and Goddess: This spirit is most powerful one. When Goddess is transmigrated severely to a person then that person died. They say the people who have a bad luck are affected by such type of spirit.

The Gunia also tries to control this spirit. But if it does not then he ties the affected person and tries to know the name of Goddess. After knowing the name, he sacrifices animals to which the Goddess prefers. Inspite of all these things if it does not control then the person become died.

The Banjara people consider that the spirit of unmarried male person is more powerful than the Chirangul. But the person affected by goddess, this spirit is powerful than all spirit.

A.7 Other Spirits: The person who died of accident, then the spirit of that person affected to people. The affected person then started trembling, his/her mouth become closed. The person is given the mixture of broom stick leaf to smell, and then the spirit goes away from the body by holding the broom stick. When a person died by sinking in water, then spirit of that person affect only to child or person who sent for bathing.

Banjara people believe the spirit enter to the body of a girl when she wears red or black dress and go outside in afternoon.

B. Good Spirits:

B.1 Ancestral Spirits: Ancestral spirits are like ghost. Ancestral spirits are generally protective and people offer them food in their name at Ishana. The Banjara people believe if their ancestral spirits angry, then to satisfy them they prepared a food namely 'Labsif' offer in their name.

B.2 Worship of Ishana Devata: It is a mound of soil present at any corner of house. On Diwali they mainly (elder person of family) pour water in the name of ancestor and offer labsif, sweets into the hearth in their names. They mainly worship 'Isana' for welfare of family.

These are all about the spirits and the concept of Banjara people.

Banjara's Idea of Sin

- For them when a girl love to a boy or when a sister has sex relation with her brother or father then they do not see their face, do not take meal from their hands. They take an egg and try to put into their nose and beat with shoes. This is equal for both male and female persons. They throw that person from their caste. It is a great sin for them.

- When a girl touches their God and Goddess during her menstrual period, then they sacrifice animal in the name of God or Goddess. It is also a great sin for them.
- When a person kills a cow, it is a sin.
- The boys and girls having sexual relation with one another, mostly separated from their caste. But when they become bald, invite village people and give sweets, rice, dal, roti etc. then the Nayak and Brahman come and sprinkle milk over them, then only they can again enter into their caste.

Restriction on Females

Females are not allowed to eat goat, sheep and swan meat. After attaining maturity they are not allowed to eat.

Various auspicious and suspicious symbols

Banjara people have a great faith in it. They believe in various auspicious and suspicious symbols such as –

- According to them when they see bird 'Tera' mainly on Bijaya dashami, it is an auspicious symbol for them.
- When a wolf passed from right to left side while walking on the road it is also good.
- Seeing a dead body, seeing an elephant on the road is also auspicious symbol.
- When the wolf passed from left to right then it is a suspicious sign for them.
- Seeing a banana tree, a Barren lady, an empty pot is an ominous sign.
- Besides all these believe they also worship various trees. To which they think as a symbol of God. These are 'pipal tree', 'Neam tree', 'Tulsi plant', 'Banyan tree', 'Amla tree', 'Kendu tree', 'gourd tree' etc.

4

ANNUAL CYCLE OF RITUALS AND FESTIVALS

> "There are always prescribed ways of carrying on religious act and procedures, ways of worshipping, praying, chanting, sacrificing, making offerings and soon, that are called rituals." *(Emile Durkheim in W.A. Lessa, 1958:134)*

INTRODUCTION

As per definition, Religion is the belief in supernatural beings. However, each society or group of people have traditional methods of controlling these powers or to subordinate them through certain actions of occultism or esoteric practices, rites, rituals and ceremonies or celebrations of accompaniment with offerings, prayer or sacrifices. So is to appease, placate or propitiate in order to enjoy a trouble freelife, rituals, rules, procedures etc. through cult or systematized celebrated rituals or manifestations. With the passage of time, these are handed down from generation to generation and are entrenched into the thickly woven fabric of culture (Tylor, 1874: 425-447).

Rituals and festivals are closely related. Festival is an organized series of special events and performances or any occasion for celebration. Annual cycle of rituals means various ritual activities during various festivals and various worship through out the year.

The religious rites and festivals associated with the agricultural cycle are not only related to the immediate practical interest of life but also evoke the emotion that goes beyond and mere to practical needs.

As the Banjara people are agriculturalists, most of the festivals are observed by them either before the cultivation or after the cultivation throughout the year.

There are various religious and magical rites ceremonies and festivals which are observed by Banjara throughout the year. Some of these festivals are connected with agricultural, while some others are observed for health and happiness of the village community. Various sacrifices are also given during these different types of festivals.

So the different festivals which are connected to the activities of Banjara people during their life times are given below.

DIFFERENT TYPES OF FESTIVALS

Of the different types of festivals, some of festivals are celebrated in family or house level whereas some are at the village level. The different festivals observed in different months are given below:

Months name in Odia	Months in English
Baisakha	April-May
Jyesta	May-June
Ashada	June-July (Ratha Yatra)

Months name in Odia	Months in English
Srabana	July-August (Rakhi,Tij, Hareliuansh)
Bhadraba	August-September (Nabanna or Nuakhai)
Aswinya	September-October (Dussehra, Balijatara, Garvana Sankranti)
Kartika	October-November (Diwali, Charu puja)
Margasira	November-December (Manabasa)
Pausa	December-January (Pausa Purnima)
Magha	January-February (Pedrani Devi Jatra
Phalguna	February-March(Holi)
Chaitra	March-April (Chaitra, Siva Ratri)

Village Level Festivals

Tij Festival: Tij festival is found in Banjara society. It is a village level or communal festival. All the villagers gather at a common place in the village and celebrate it. It is held in the month of Srabana (July-August). The Banjara people observe it for nine days. It is the worship of sand in the name of Meramaa.

Tij is the name of sand. It is sprinkled in the name of Meramaa. Only Bhukia family member can worship during this festival but he must be an unmarried one. It is held on Tuesday. The face of the Goddess is towards east.

On First Day: When they first cut their new crops and bring it home, after that they celebrate this festival. They bring sand. In the evening the Banjara people take nine types of seeds of various crops. Then they make a 'Bani' and fill this with sand. In the evening every person puts a lump of mud in this 'Bani'. Then the priest lights diya and agarbati, puts vermilion on it and does 'Namaskara'.

On Second Day: On the second day the priest worships this 'Bani' in morning. Then all girls of the village go for bath. After bathing they offer flowers to this Bani, in which sand is kept in the name of Meramma and do Namaskar.

Then on third, fourth, fifth, sixth, seventh and eighth day, they continue this process which they practice on the second day. On all these days this 'Bani' is worshipped by priest in the morning. For nine days, they sprinkle water on the 'Bani'.

On Ninth Day: On all these days including the ninth day, all the boys and girls dance every morning and evening. On the ninth day, the boys hold 'Gedi' and girls hold 'Bhala' and the girl beat the boy's 'Gedi'. This occurs in the afternoon.

Tenth day is the last day of the festival. They sacrifice a male brown goat on this day. All the people take part in this feast. They all eat this meat and dance from morning to evening. Then, in the evening the boys and girls immerse the 'Gedi and Bhala' and also the Bani. In the Bani, there are sprouts from the grains previously kept, to which they do Namaskara and immerse in the water.

This is all about Tij festival, which is mainly observed for the welfare of village and for more production of grains or crops from the land.

Hareliuansh: It is also another communal festival which is also observed to increase the fertility of land. Banjara people have different types of beliefs, due to which they practice different rituals and observe different festivals.

This festival held once in a year i.e the month of Srabana (July-August). On this festival all the male members, both married and unmarried, take a 'karama branch' dug out of the root of the rice grains in the agriculture field. It is also practiced by Hindu society. Then there is a place on the land called as 'Gudi', where sacrifices are done. Mainly black cock and coconut are given. They first offer flowers and then put namaskara and after that sacrifice animal. Then they arrange a feast there and all the members of villagers come there to take part in the feast. They observe this festival before the grains start growing. They have a belief that by observing this festival the paddy will grow better.

Dussehra: Dussehra is the main festival of Banjara. Banjara people observe Dussehra in the month of Aswinna (September-October). People celebrate this festival at village level. During this time people do not go to the crop fields. The houses are cleaned with a mixture of water and cowdung solution. Then the worship starts.

In very early times they observed Dussehra for ten days. But now they observe it only for one day mainly on Dashami. In Dabriguda village, all people gather at 'Gountia' house to discuss how to do the worship in a proper way. In the morning they worship Danteswari. She is worshipped by the elder member of 'Gountia' family. Women are not allowed to witness the Puja. But they can arrange all materials needed for worship. They clean that place, arrange various types of flowers etc. Then the male members worshipped to Danteswari and Ashawari. They sacrifice pumpkin, fruits and brown male goat to Danteswari and black goat to Ashawari. Then in the afternoon, all the people arrange a feast of the sacred offals. In the evening that day, all the male members bring talwar, dhal and make a turban. They put this turban on the head and go to worship Danteswari. After coming back home, the ladies put Tilak on the male members' forehead. The tilak is a mixture of turmeric and rice. They do Arati of the male members. All the people sit together with their elder members. The seniors give advice to the juniors. Then they take 'Kuliari' leaf and put it at the two sides of ear. They do Namaskara to all the members. They take the sacred offals. The Brahmin priest gives 'Pitrusarat' to their ancestor.

They have a belief that on Vijaya-dashami their ancestors won in war and came back home. So to remember this day they celebrate Dussehra, especially the Dashami in a very great manner.

Diwali: Diwali is celebrated by all Banjara people in the month of Kartika (October-November). Earlier, they observed Diwali for two days. But now they observe it only for one day.

On First day: On the first day of Diwali, they do Laxmi Puja. It is mainly done by married female members. The priest is of Brahmin caste. They keep paddy near Laxmi Devi and worship her. All members do it combinedly. They do not sacrifice any animals. They don't take non-vegetarian food.

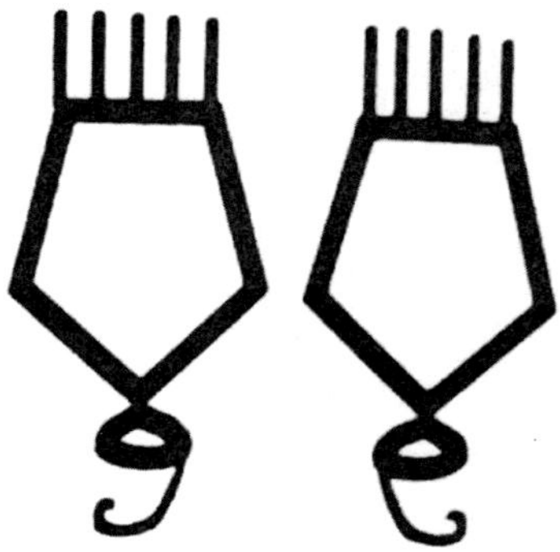

At first they clean the houses with cow dung. Then draw a Laxmi's foot, by art. Then a 'Mana' (a pot) is decorated with art and the females fill 'Paddy' in that Mana. Then all these are put on a raised platform called 'Pidha'. The 'Pidha' is also cleaned by cow dung solution. Flowers are used for decoration and a clean cloth is covered over the 'mana'. Then this is worshipped as a symbol of Laxmi Devi, or in some cases they worship the photo of Laxmi Devi.

Then they prepare a Jhoti from rice powder and make symbols using the Jhoti in front of the 'Mana'. This is also done every Thursday in front of house. They think of these symbols to be a representation of Laxmi Devi. Then they take sacred offals of Laxmi Devi.

On Second day: This is the most special day. On this day they do Gobardhan Puja. Female members also do this. All the married ladies gather at one place; they clean a place with cow dung solution. Then they make a mound of cowdung, three cubes of cow dung over the mound. Then over these three are put over other three cubes of cow dung. Then they put paddy and flowers on each cow dung gola. Then they put adiya in middle of all golas. The diya is hand-made with rice powder, which has been boiled in water. In the diya, they put ghee and sacred stick and light it. The face of this is towards east and it is covered by cloth. Then they sprinkle curd, milk, and rice powder around this mound.

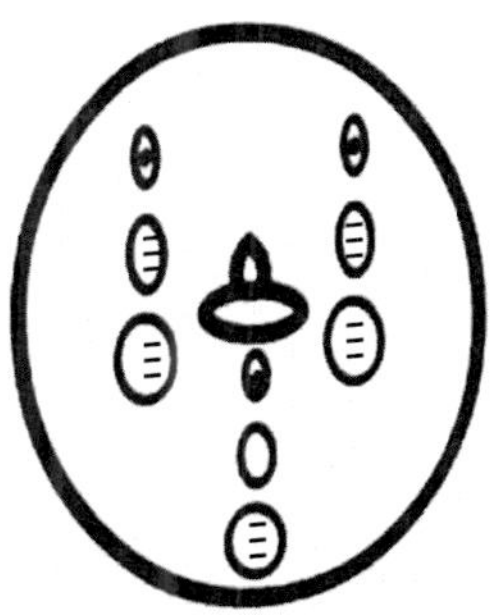

Then they invite the priest to worship. The priest is a female member. She fasts the whole day and worships this mound by offering flowers, coconut and various fruits. Then all members take blessings. On Diwali all the people also worship the cow. Then at night they decorate their house with sacred flame and celebrate Diwali.

On the next morning they go for bath and after that they worship cow. At the time of bathing they give water to 'Ushributa' plant. They put cow dung, one rupee, and milk near the root of the 'Ushributa' plant. Then they give rice and flower in the name of their ancestors and return home. They very interestingly observed this in ancient times.

But now with the impact of modernization, all these customs are destroyed. Diwali is not observed for two days. Now, on Diwali, they do Laxmi Puja in morning and Gobardhan puja in the evening. They observes Diwali mainly for welfare of cows and accumulation of wealth.

5. Holi: Holi is another festival. Banjara people observe it for three days. It is observed in the month of phalguna (February-March). All Banjara people combinedly observe this festival.

First day: On the first day, all people play with mud among themselves.Then they take bath and eat various tasty foods which are purely vegetarian. This is called as "Sukla bhoga".

Second day: On the second day they eat non-vegetarian foods and play 'phagu' among themselves.

Third day: On third day they prepare various types of foods and eat them. When they play phagu, all the people play togathered. But the males and females play separately. They play 'phagu' with each other in their different age group. Before they play 'phagu', they bring a piece of wood from their house. Then all the woods are gathered near the 'Mahula' tree. There is wooden tomb near mahula tree which they worship as Holika Devi. Around this tomb they gather all the woods and light a fire. All this takes place in morning and requires only the male members. Then they play phagu in the afternoon. In the evening the boys and girls take 'panchamruta' for seven times and sing songs. Then they go around the mahula tree mainly around the tomb and returned home. Only the second day, they eat non-vegetarian foods and worship Holika Devi. Black or red cocks and sheep are sacrificed by the village priest. After that they arranged a feast with the sacrificed offal. Then all members come and eat. This worship is done for the welfare of the village.

6. Pausa Purnima: It is the most important and interesting festival of Banjara. It is held in the month of Pausa (December-January). All girls get up from bed very early. It is celebrated combinedly. Female members clean the house and wash it with cow dung. The unmarried girls go to the pond. Then they worship Jalakamini. It is held in the month of pausa and in full Moon day. Therefore it is called as pausa purnima. They first take bath, then they take a pot and mix jaggery with water and offer it in the name of Jalakamini. Then they offer flowers and agarbati to her and come back to home. Then they wear new dress and sing song 'Cher Chera' and go to each house of village to collect some money or rice. They arranged a feast with the collected amount. But they do not eat non-vegetarian food on this day. Then they invite all boys of their village. At last, girls are given sweets to eat. This is a new year celebration for them.

7. Chaitra: Chaitra festival/ritual is observed by Banjara people in the month of Chaitra (March-April) on Tuesday.

Banjara worship Gudiani, Thakurani and Barsarmajhi on this festival. These three Goddess are village Goddess. The symbol of these Goddess comes out from one house and goes to each house of village. The houses to which the symbol goes, the members of that house worship and offer flowers, coconut etc.

Then this symbol is taken to the temple of village. It is the temple of this Goddess. Women carry this symbol. Then the Devi is transmigrated to the people who carried the symbol. To which they called as 'Devi Kheliba' or it is called as 'sira kheliba'. To which all members ask about their problems. That person can solve anybody's problem. Before the transmigration of Devi, the symbol is worshiped by priest and also to these three Goddess. The person who has asked for something to these Goddess and it is fulfilled, then that person can only take that symbol. Then they sacrifice pigeon and goat in front of the symbol and Goddess. After that all people come back home and arrange a great feast with the sacrificed animals. This festival is observed mainly for the over all welfare of the village.

8. Balijatara: The festival is observed in the month of Chaitra (March-April). They observe it in a very great manner. It is observed for nine days. Girls mainly observe Balijatara. But they fast only for one day.

On the first day morning, they carry sand after bathing from river. At night they take green gram (moong dal), rice, black gram (biri), mustard and incense stick (bati) and the sand and put all these in a pot. Then they make 5 to 7 pots made up of soil and put all these items inside all these pots. They make it in the name of their God, Goddess, or their brother. Upto ninth day they sprinkle turmeric water on it.

The sand becomes swollen and looks like yellow colour. On the eighth day the girl listens to Veda and Sastra. On 9th day they take this pot and tear a part of that sacred stick inside. Then they give it to their brother to put this thread around their neck, which consists of eight nodes. This is called as 'bhai jeeti' by Banjara. Then all the girls take the pot and float it in the river.

After that the girls take their lunch. But during these nine days they do not take non-vegetarian food items. On the first day the girls do not take any meal. This festival is observed mainly by unmarried girls. For nine days, the pot is worshipped by only Brahmin priest. But all the arrangements are done by the girls. On this day the girls do not take any meal. They take 'Nakachana' and put it in water. Then the 'Nakachana' becomes swollen due to the water. Then they prick it in each thorn of berry tree. Then after they become pure and can take meal but the boys try to impure it by spitting.

This is also a village level festival. In Hanspada village the 'Bhukia' worships in Balijatara festival. The name of Bhukia is Judhistira Naik. After the death of main Bhukia, any member of his family can worship. In absence of any member they call Bhukia from other village.

Family or Clan Level Festivals

1. Rakhi purnima: Banjara people observe different types of festivals, which they observe at family level. From those Rakhi purnima is one. It is celebrated in the month of Srabana (July-August). It is a Hindu festival.

On this day, in the morning, the girls first take bath. Then they prepare a tilak of sandal and vermilion. Then in a plate they put 'Arua Chaula' with the sandal and vermillion mixture and diya in front of the brother. Then they put the tilak on the brother's forehead and tie the rakhi. Then they sprinkle the 'arua chaula' and take Arati. After that the brother will give some gift (may be rupees, dress etc.) to the sister. It is observed by both married and unmarried person. They observe it for the long live of their brother. On this day they prepare cake, labsif to eat and also invite various guests to their houses.

Before doing all these things they first take 'aruachaula', flowers and sprinkle water and then tie Rakhi to the land in morning. They believe this rakhi is given to Goddess Laxmi. Then tied to their brothers.

It shows a great attachment and affection to the agricultural land.

2. Nabanna: They also observe this festival. It is celebrated in the month of Bhadraba (August-September). It is also called as 'Nuakhai' in Hindu society.

When they cut their grain, after that they celebrate this festival. They first clean the houses with cow dung. The female members play a great role in this festival. It is observed in family or clan level. Women in the morning take bath and prepare labsif with the new grains. It is prepared as follows. They first grind rice, after that boil it in water and added jaggery or sugar in it and mix it. Then it becomes very thick. It is also very easy to prepare, then the women of the house prepare cake, sweets, dal, curry etc. The women also wear a new sari on this occasion.

Then the head household lady offers these items first into the hearth in the name of their ancestors. Then she offers it at

'Isana Devata' for the ancestral deity. Then they worship their 'Ista Devi'. After that all family members eat together.

In this festival non-vegetarian food is strictly prohibited. Nabanna occurs mainly on Friday or Wednesday. In this festival, ladies also have a great role.

3. Garvana Sankranti: It is another family level festival. It occurs in the month of Aswina (September-October) just after Dussehra.

On this day the Banjara people do not go to the fields. They don't do any work on this day. They believe that land is Laxmi Devi and rice come out of it and they think Laxmi is pregnant in this month.Therefore, they do not cultivate any thing during this month and worship the land on this day. This worship is done at the time when seeds are in the land. They, mainly the female members, take a pot, put vermilion on it and also take sandal and some paddy in it. Then they worship Laxmi Devi at home and prepare a 'panchamruta' (they call it panchiamruta). It is the mixture of ghee, jaggery, curd, honey and milk. Then the Banjara people get blessing and take the panchamruta. After that the male members take it to the land and sprinkle it, after the spreading of seeds. Each person worships for his or her own land.

They do all these rituals and festivals by seeing the calendar (panji).

4. Charu Puja: It occurs in the month of Kartika (October-November). This worship also occurs at family level mainly on Tuesday. This worship occurs just after the sowing of seeds. They first worship the ploughing machine. The male member, mainly elder people of the family cleans the machine and washes it. Then the female members bring vermilion and coconut. The elder person first marks by vermilion on the ploughing machine and breaks a coconut in front of it.

Then they go to land put agarbati in soil and vermilion and break coconut on the land. Then they sacrifice black cock or any bird. This is done facing towards west. This is called as 'Rakta Bhoga'. This worship is called as Charu Puja.

After that they arrange a feast of the sacrificed animals near the land. They also invite their near and dear friends. This worship is done to grow grains more quickly and to protect it from any disease.

5. Manabasa: It is held in the month of Margasira (November-December). Married female member do this on Thursday. It is a festival of the Hindu society.

The houses are cleaned with cow dung and all the utensils of the house are washed. Then in a clean room, a basket full of paddy is placed. Around this various types of art and Laxmi's foot is made with rice powder. Then they place it on a 'pidha'. After that a married women worship this. She does fast all the day. Then puts vermilion mark on this basket and sprinkles cow dung solution all over it. Then gives flowers and lights agarbati and diya in front of it. After that she breaks the coconut and all the members of the house take blessings of the Goddess.

Then all members take sacred offal. On this day nobody can take non-vegetarian food. They mainly observe this festival for the peace of house and for lots of wealth.

6. Pedrani Devi Jatra: It is held in the month of Magha (January-February). It mainly occurs on Panchami. It is also a houselevel worship.

In this festival, they perform the pedrani Devi Puja in a very great manner. First in morning they wash the houses and purify it by sprinkling the cow dung solution. Female members of the family do this.

They consider Pedrani Devi as an arrow with a basket covered with a red cloth, which is full of shells, which they worship. The worship is done mainly by the eldest person in the family. He must not eat anything from morning. This Puja starts mainly in the afternoon after 3-4 pm. The person doing the puja takes red hibiscus, vermilion, and lights diya and agarbatti in front of the Devi. Then he sacrifices a male goat and offers a lemon and coconut in front of her.

Then all family members arrange feast of the sacrificed animal and invite their close relatives to a feast in the evening. It is mainly done for family welfare. After a heavily labored agricultural season, they take rest and enjoy this Jatra very much.

7. **Siva Ratri:** It is also a Hindu festival. But as Banjara people live near Hindu people so most of their culture is mixed with the Hindu culture.

It is held in the month of phalguna (February-March). They have a Siva temple at their village end. So in this temple they worship Lord Siva. Siva Ratri it is also called as 'jagara'. All the people fast on this day. They only take fruits or water. Then in the evening they go to Siva temple with diya, ghee and agarbati. Brahmin priest does this worship. Then the people take some food after the 'Mahadipa' mainly after 11-12 P.M. at night. In this festival male and female members take part together.

These are the various festivals observed by the Banjara people.

WORSHIP OF VARIOUS DEITIES

Banjara of Dabriguda village worship different deities. Different persons of the village worship these deities.

1. Banjari Devi

Materials required–Vermilion, brown goat, flowers, 'singli', 'kapadia', 'mayura', 'chandrika', a rope with bell, white cock, coconut etc.

At first mainly in Dussehra they worship Banjari Devi. First (the stone) to which they think as Banjari Devi is worshipped by 'Nayak' (village chief) of the village. Nayak has a great personality. In village every person admires him. He controls all the works related to political, religious, social and economic activities. Banjari Devi is placed under 'Mahula' tree at village end. Then mainly on Dussehra the 'Nayak' after bathing wears a dhoti and puts a apron on his body. Then he sprinkles water on the sacred place, puts vermilion over the stone and puts flowers over it. Then he lights some agarbati and prostrates in front of the deity. His face is towards East direction and all sacrifices are also done in this direction. Then they sacrifice brown goat in front of her. They first wash it with water. Then put a vermilion mark on its forehead and sacrifice the got, some elder persons of village and 'Nayak' also go to assist in sacrificing animal. Banjara people before going to marry also worship in the name of Banjari Devi. When the bride-groom goes for marriage, the 'Nayak' and some members of that family go with him and worship Banjari Devi. Only male members are allowed. After worshipping Banjara Devi, they worship the bulls during Dussehra. They place 'ladan' at the backside of bull and give a vermilion mark on its forehead. They adorn 'singli' to bull in his horn, 'Kapadia' to its face and 'Mayura chandrika' (peacock feather) is attached to the horn of bull. A rope with bell is hanged around his neck. Male members of the village decorate the bull this way. Then the 'Nayak' strikes coconut in front of bull. Then all village people take the bull out of the village and bring it back. Then the 'Nayak' sacrifice a white cock in front of the bull. The sacrifice is done in front of the bull facing toward east direction. The face of Banjari Devi is also towards east. Then with the sacrifice of animals they arrange a great feast. In which all the villages participate except the female members of village. In Hanspada village the name of 'Nayak' is Kuna Naik.

Swarga Maili

Swarga Maili is worshipped on the hilltop. The Banjaras worship Swarga Maili mainly for rain. The deity is especially worshipped by Banjara people.

Materials Required: Diya, agarbati, white pigeon, paddy, black goat, flowers, vermilion etc.

It is a village level worshipping. When it does not rain for quite some time, all the villagers fix a day. For this date they consult an auspicious book called 'Panji' by referring the matter to Nayak. Then mainly on Tuesday, all the male members of the village take bath in the morning and prepare themselves. They bring a priest from other village. It is the worship of two to three villages. Then mainly married person with the priest goes to the mountain, beating the drum. There on the hilltop is a 'footprint' which they worship as

'Swarga Maili'. The priest sprinkles water over it. Then puts vermilion on the footprint and lights diya and agarbati infront of it. Then the priest offers red Hibiscus flowers and paddy to the foot print. After all this is done, the priest sacrifices a white pigeon (male) and a black goat (male) in front of the Devi. Then they all take blessing and pray for rain.

After doing all the rituals the priest covers the print by 'duguri'. Then all people come back to the village and arrange a feast with the sacred offals. All over the year the 'footprint' is covered by duguri. Only on this day it is opened for a while, then again closed by the priest.

3. Mati Devi

Banjaras also worship Mati Devi. The various materials required for Mati Devi's are given below:

Materials required: Coconut, agarbati, red flowers, wine, vermilion, pig, brown male goat etc.

Mati Devi temple is situated at the village end facing towards west. Village priest faces towards east direction and worships it. He first takes bath, then on empty stomach he puts on dhoti and does puja. After that he, along with few elder members of village go to the temple. He takes all the materials needed for worship. He first sprinkles water at the place of Devi. They called at place as 'Devir Asana'. Then the priest offers flowers, light diya and agarbati. After that he breaks coconut in front of the Devi. He also offers wine to her. Then all the members do Namaskara.

After that there is a place where animals are sacrificed infront of her. They sacrifice pig, brown male goat in front of her towards east direction. But they do not eat this meat. In most of their festivals mainly male members are allowed.

She is worshipped on every Tuesday. Only on this day the temple is open, otherwise it is always closed.

4. Danteswari

She is a very famous Banjara deity. The large majority of Banjara people also consider her as their presiding deity. The materials required for her worship are given below.

Materials required: Rice powder, Milk, Agarbati, yellow Zinnia flower, red Hibiscus, brown goat, black cock etc.

The name of the priest of Nayakpada is 'Bhagirathi Cahaa'. He is the Nayak (head man) of village. Danteswari is worshipped along with Lukudia. Both are kept facing toward each other in the middle of village.

In the month of Dussehra, mainly on Dashami, the priest first takes bath in morning. Then wears dhoti and he goes to the place of worship. Before he starts worship, the women first polish the ground surface by cowdung. Then they make a ritual symbol of Danteswari with rice powder on the polished surface. Then the priest starts worship. He first sprinkles water around the 'Large Bhat' to which they refer as Danteswari. Then he sprinkles milk on it. Then he

puts vermilion on the vermilion mark point, lights agarbati and offers red hibiscus flowers to the Devi. Special preferences given to yellow zinnia flower for this worship. Then the priest sacrifices brown male goat or cock in front of her. Then again the priest sprinkles water for the cooling of Devi's anger as they imagine. Then all do Namaskara. The priest distributes the prasad. While doing Puja the face of priest is towards west direction and sacrifices are also given in this direction.

Then the worship of Lukudia starts. The ground surface is also plastered with cowdung in and around the deity. Then the priest sprinkles water and offers red hibiscus to him facing towards west direction. Lukudia is the male deity. He helps Danteswari. Then brown goat and cock is also sacrificed in front of him facing toward west direction. At last the priest also sprinkles water over the deity for his satisfaction and calmness.

Then all members arrange feast with these sacrificed animals and eat combinely. The worship starts at 9 A.M. and continue still 7-8 P.M. at night. The post of priest is hereditary and elder son of the priest has right to become priest after the death or inability of the former priest.

5. *Phulamauli*

The Banjara people worship Phulamauli for increasing fertility of soil and also success in fishing.

Materials required: Black powder, red powder, rice powder, flowers, agarbati, big male goat.

In the month of Chaitra, (March-April) they worship Phulamauli. All the male members participate in it. It is worshipped by the elder person of family. In Dabriguda village all people have their own land. So each family worships separately in their own land.

From the early morning the priest takes bath. He does

not eat any thing till the worship is complete. When it is evening, the priest along with 2-3 members of village goes to the land. There is a remarkable place where the symbol of Devi is placed. The priest first sprinkles water over it by uttering mantras. Then puts vermilion on the vermilion marked points, and then he offers black powder, rice powder and flowers over it. After that he lights agarbati in front of her. Then he sacrifices big male goat there in the name of Phulamauli. If she is satisfied then the fertility of soil automatically increases. Then all members come back home and the priest takes some food but it must be vegetarian food.

6. Ritual Practices for rain

As Kalahandi district is a drought affected area, there is a huge scarcity of water. So in Dabriguda village if it has no rain, then in the month of march-April, all Banjara people both men and women gather in the middle of village.The village priest is called to worship. The village priest may be of Gond tribe or schedule caste person. The priest first takes bath, wears dhoti, puts a tilak on his forehead and comes tothe villlage. Then he first offers flowers in the name of Barsarmajhi, Thakurani and Basterein. Then he strikes a coconut on the ground in their name. All the people gather here. Women are allowed to arrange various materials required for this worship.

Then the priest sacrifices pig in their name. After that they have a belief, it will automatic rain. Inspite of this ritual if it does not rain, then they do 'Kirtana' in the month of November-December.

7. Thakurani

The temple of Thakurani is present outside of village.

Materials required: Vermillion, agarbati, red hibiscus, pumpkin, black goat (male).

This temple is opened mainly on Chaitra, Chittalagi Amabasya and Dussehra. Only the Priest opens the temple on these occasions, which otherwise remains closed.

Mainly in Dussehra or Chittalagi Amabasya, the village priest after taking bath, completing all his works, goes to the temple of Thakurani. He has an assistant to assist him with his work. He then opens the temple and sprinkles water all over the area. There is a symbol of Thakurani. The priest sits in front of Godess, then offers vermilion and flowers to Devi. He offers Diya and Agarbati to her. When he sits in front of Devi, his face is toward east, the Devi is on one side of the temple. They call the Devi as 'Thakuranigudi'. Then they sacrifice pumpkin and male black goat infront of Devi, sacrifices are also done facing east direction. The face of Devi is toward west. Other Goddesses like Pardeshan, Manpuren, and Maakalika are also with Thakurani in that temple.

Thakurani Devi has her own dress. The person to whom Maa is transmigrated, that person wears this specific dress. There is a swing in which a number of pins are stuck. The person also sits on that swing and he himself pricks trishul into his body. The person may be a male or female one. All these show that when a Devi is transmigrated to a person, nothing unfortunate happens to him.

8. Talja bhabani

Mainly the Bhukia, Ortia, Kelut clan people worship Talja Bhabani.

Materials required: Rice powder, flowers, agarbati, and brown goat.

Mainly Banjara worships Danteswari in the month of October, during Dussehra. On Dashami morning, the houses are cleaned and plastered with cow dung solution. Both men and women take bath in the morning. Then the head of the Banjara family gets ready. Before that the women first clean the materials required for puja. Then the male members go into the 'Devata ghar'. The priest first sprinkles water all over, then lights diya and agarbati. After that he offers flowers and vermilion to it. All of them form a ritual diagram of Talja-bhabani by rice powder 'arua chaula'. In each block they put some pinch of rice powder. These three blocks are for Talja-bhabani. After completing the puja, sacrifices are given. A brown male goat is sacrificed. The face of priest is also towards west in front of Devi whose face is towards east.

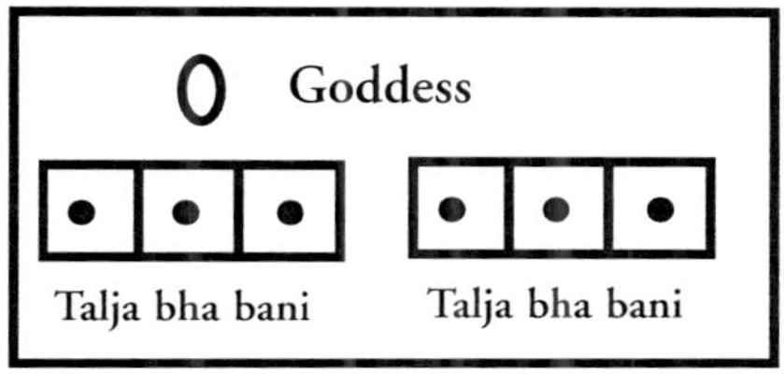

After completing all these, the villagers arrange a feast with the sacrifice animal. Women are also allowed to eat the offal.

9. Pedrani Devi

Materials required: Rice, red hibiscus, Muhan, agarbati, zinnia, lemon, coconut, black male goat.

Pedrani Devi is worshipped once in every 15 days. The elder member of the family worships her. The name of priest is Durya Naik. They have a separate room which is different from their usual rooms in which they have kept Pedrani Devi. The worship starts at 3 P.M. and continue still 5 P.M. The pujari doesn't eat non-vegetarian food on this day. It occurrs mainly on Sundays. He can take fruits. After completion of worship he can take his meal but only vegetarian food. The priest first sprinkles water, then sits in front of the Devi, facing towards East. They put a cane stick at the side of Devi's crown, a 'nigama' an axe is placed in front of Devi. They believe the person into who Maa is transmigrated, that person will beat everyone with the nigama and solve every body's problem. The priest, after sprinkling water, puts vermilion on its marked point then offers flowers at the foot of Devi and lights agarbati in front of her. After that the priest offers lemon to Devi in banana leaf and then beats coconut in front of her. Then the priest sprinkles again water over all these things to cool it. Then hedoes namaskara to Devi. Some people also offer 'liya' to Devi and then they ring a bell. Then the Devi is transmigrated to a self-chosen person.

But the Banjara people believe that Pedrani Maa doesn't want sacrifice. But her nine soldiers want sacrifice. Among them Jhit is one, the gate keeper of police station. But now he is in Maa's room. Kalarein is another soldier of Pedrani Devi. Only they want sacrifice. Therefore, black goat is sacrificed in front of them. Nigaman and Luagayinee are also the soldiers of Pedrani Devi. So the Jhit, Kalarein, Nigman and Luagayinee, these four are in front of Devi facing towards East. But the Devi's face is towards west. Sacrifices are given towards west direction.

After that all members take the sacred offal of Pedrani Devi.

10. Charukhuta

Materials required: Black cock, vermilion, red hibiscus etc.

The Banjara people also worship Charukhuta. This worship occurs on the agricultural land. The elder members of the family worship it. The priest after bathing in morning along with other members of the family goes to the land. Here he first sprinkles water to purify that place. Then he offers Vermilion and Red hibiscus to the Devi. After that he lights agarbati. He sits in front of Devi (whose face is towards East) facing towards west. Then they sacrifice black cock in front of Devi, in west direction. This is mainly done on Tuesday or Thursday, when half of paddy is cut from the land or before cutting the crops.

11. *Isana Devata*

The Banjara people also worship Isana Devata. The name of the priest is 'Parmananda Naik'. The Isana is placed in the one corner of kitchen. On Diwali and various other occasions, they worship 'Isana'. On any special occasion, females of family wash houses with cow dung solution. Then the priest worships the Isana Devata. The face of 'Isana' is towards East. While worshipping, the face of priest is towards west. On Diwali the priest pours water in the name of the family ancestor. They also cooked food, labsif, sweets and it is offered near Ishana in their ancestor's name. No sacrifices are given to this deity; only agarbati, vermilion and flowers are given while worshipping before any festive occasion.

All Banjara people have a belief that by worshipping Isana, they can lead a peaceful life. It is mainly observed for the welfare of the family.

12. *Full dark night (Uansh)*

On this day all Banjara people inside a 'lota' or pot, put dal, ghee, jaggery, axe etc and sprinkle cow dung solution 'gorous'. Every household member does this worship mainly on full dark night. Male members of the family mainly do it.

All these are about the various ritual activities practices during the worship of different deities.

13. Fullmoon Night (Puneei)

On full moon night, all women worship it.It is a worship of Chand or moon by amla. Bale leaves, ghee, jaggery, thread, tumeric and paddy is offer to him. It is mainly done by female members of family.

All these are about the various ritual activities practices during the worship of different deities.

RITUAL DIAGRAM

Besides all these Diagrams, Banjara people also do some other ritual diagram during the worshipping of different deities and during different festivals. In the worship of Meramaa they draw this diagram with rice powder.

Various Symbols

- The laudia clan people at the backside of their cow draw this type of symbol to recognize their cow.

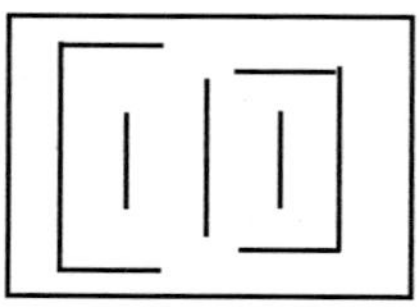

- Island clan people form this symbol at the left side of leg of cow to recognize as their cow.

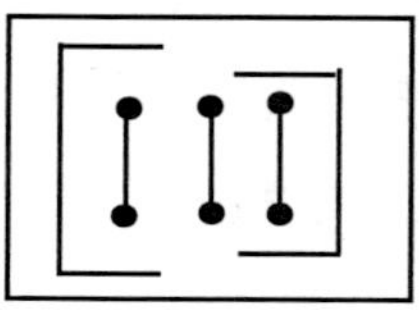

But they do not have such symbol on goats. If they see such symbol on a goat, they treat it like a cow and don't eat its meat.

- Rathod clan people draw a line above the nose of cow.
- Kelut clan people draw this symbol on the lower part of stomach. The bending lines as draw in diagram meet at the trunk. By seeing this they recognize their cow.
- **For Spirit:** Mainly it is formed by turmeric powder, black powder, vermilion, white powder. They form seven blocks and in each blockput a little amount of rice above which seven different types of flowers are put in seven blocks.

RITUAL FRIENDSHIP

A case study from the village Dabriguda about ritual friendship is collected.

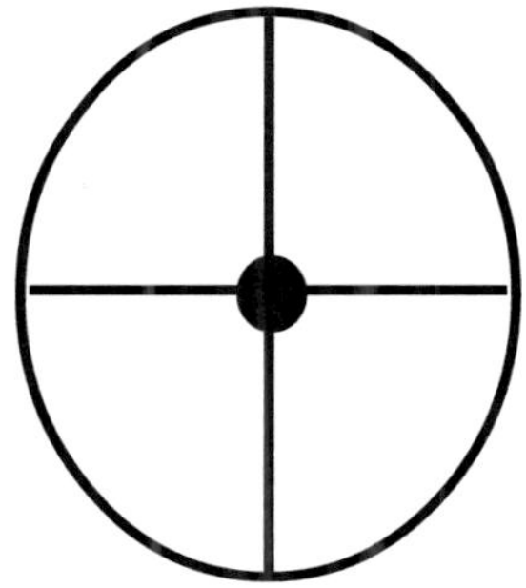

Lata and Puspa sat together as Makara or 'Gajamung'. In Tij festival they first light diya in front of the 'Bani'. They both bring coconuts and parents of both of the girls are present there. Then both the girls hold each other's ears. From that day onwards, they call each other as 'Gajamung' or Makara.

This is a ritual friendship found in Banjara society. But it is perhaps influenced from Hindu society.

Another case study is taken from Jaipal Naik. He said, they can sit 'makara' with any body other than their Banjara caste. But boys can make 'makara' only to boys and girls can make only to girls. If they made 'makara' with other caste then they follow some restriction. Whatever festivals they observe; they first invite their 'makara'. They separately cook for 'makara'. In marriage and death ritual also 'makara' is invited. They do not quarrel with 'makara'. The food they prepare for 'makara' is called as 'Mahaprasad'. They do this with affection as they want to keep this relationship life long and not qarrel with everybody and make everyone their friend. So to mention this they make "Mahaprasad for Makara".

Besides all these, Banjara worship pipal tree on Saturday for satisfaction of planet (Graha Shanti) and worship Banyan tree on Sunday for child.

List

Name of Deities	The Worshipper
Banjari Devi	Nayak
Charu Khuta	Elder member of family
Danteswari	Nayak
Daragadhiani	Village Priest
Jalakamini	Married woman
Kali Devi	Brahmin Priest
Laxmi Puja	Married women or Brahmn Priest
Lukudia	Nayak
Mati Devi	Village Priest. (oriya priest)
Matrala	Nayak
Meramaa	A member of Rathod family (unmarried)
Phula Mauli	Elder person of family
Pir	Elder person of the family
Swargamaili	Nayak
Trinath mela	Bhramin priest

5

LIFE CYCLE RITUAL

> Religion is the virtue by which men show God due worship and reverence.
>
> –*Thomas Aquinas*

According to Beals and Hoijer, "Ritual is a prescribed way of performing religious act that is of praying, singing sacred songs, dancing to God, making sacrifices or preparing offering. A ceremony on the other hand involves a number of inter connected and related rituals."

INTRODUCTION

The term ritual denotes those aspects of prescribed formal behavior that have no direct technological consequences. The 'Prescription' or prescribed component in the definition, is ordinarily provided by cultural tradition but it may in some cases be a spontaneous invention of the individual. Therefore, the majority of 'religious' and 'magical' actions are ritual in this sense. Ritual actions are 'symbolic' in that they assert something about the state of affairs, but they are not necessarily purposive, that is the performer of ritual does not necessarily seek to alter the state of affairs.

According to Raymond Firth, Ritual is 'a kind of patterned activity oriented towards control of human affairs, primarily symbolic in character with non empirical reference and asarule socially sanctioned.'

Ritual expresses the personality, act, relationship, status and the way in which one behaves with others in most parts of the world.

According to Durkheim ritual has four functions namely disciplinary and preparatory, cohesive, revitalizing and europic.

For anthropologists and ecclesiastics, the term Ritual always refers to social customs, traditionally sanctioned, but some psycho-analytic writers use the term to include some prescribed and elaborated behavior that has been spontaneously invented by an individual, as by compulsion neurotics, for example. Van Gennep analyses rites de passage. There are two types of rites:

(1) Rites that accompany the passage of a person from one social status to another in the course of his or her life and,

(2) Rites that mark recognized points in the passage of time (New Year, new moon, solstice or equinox). (Mircea eliade, 1987: 308)

The term has come to be restricted to the former type, which are now sometimes called 'life-crisis rites'. Typical rites de passage in the modern sense is those that accompany, birth, the attainment of adult status, marriage and death.

Ritual is observed at planting, first fruits, harvest and other important occasion on the annual round of work. Chapple and coon have called these ceremonial rites of intensification. The acting out the habitual relation has the effect of reinforcing or intensifying their habitual relation and thus series to maintain their conditioned responses. In the technical sense the performance of these rites prevent the extinction of habits to which the individual has been trained (Edward Norbeck, 1961: 98).

Van Gannep analyzed these rites into a sequence of three stages:

(1) rites of separation,

(2) marginal or liminal rites,

(3) rites of aggregation or more simply rites of entry into, waiting in and leaving the intermediate no man's land.

The three elements are not equally marked in all rites de passage, according to Van Gennep, the element of separation is more important in mortuary or funerary rites, that of aggregation in marriage. The marginal rites, marking the period in which an individual is detached from one status but not yet admitted into the next, are most conspicuous in those initiation ceremonies that involve the participants in a long period of isolation, cut off from their normal social contact (Mircea Eliade, 1987: 386).

Life cycle rituals are category of rituals that mark in the life cycle of a person, from one stage to another over time, from one role or social position to another, integrating the human and cultural experiences with biological destiny: birth, reproduction and death. These ceremonies make the basic distinctions, observed in all groups, between young and old male and female, living and dead. This is through rites of passage that we are able to contemplate, to formulate and reformulate our ambivalent condition of animal and human. Biology dictates the fundamentals of our experience – birth, reproduction and death. Yet the ways in which we manipulate and modify these imperatives through cultural means are endless (Ibid.1987: 380).

Status A　　　　Status B
↓　　　　　　　↓
Separation ⟶ Incorporation
Transition

Various ritual activities are marked in Banjara society which are given below.

BIRTH RITUAL

Banjara people attach a lot of importance to the occasion of child birth. This is expressed in the observance of an elaborate ritual. But before the performance of birth ritual, the pregnant women go through some restrictions. Birth of baby usually occurs after nine months of development in the mother's womb. As most of the people believe the pregnant women have to wear 'tabij', before the birth of child for the purpose of protection and well being. After the birth of a baby they take it out from the mother's body. The pregnant women during pregnancy period are not allowed to go anywhere. The birth of a child usually occurs in the husband's house. The pregnant woman during her delivery time, kept in a separate room. The male members are not allowed to this room at the time of delivery. There is no restriction of food for the mother before birth of child. The woman can worship God but can't offer flowers, fruits, etc. to the God.

Banjara people believe that the woman has a fruit in her stomach and it is the gift of God. During ancient times, the birth of child occurred with the help of elder women in the family. But now they take the help of 'dhai', a trained mid-wife. But, in very serious condition of the mother or child, they go to the hospital. But they do not performance any specific ritual for the pregnant lady or during the pregnancy period of a woman. But the pregnant woman does not eat any roasted things like roasted potato, brinjal. She also does not go anywhere after evening.

On 7th Day- (Chutuka): The mother, newly born child and the 'dhai' up to seven days observe this pollution. They call it as 'chutuka'. The mother and child do not come out of the separate room. They are not allowed to worship deities during these seven days. The pregnant women does not touch water, go to kitchen. She is not allowed to take curd, tamarind within these days. She does not take bath and nobody washes her clothes.

But on the seventh day, the Banjara people, mainly all the family members wash their clothes and house with the mixture of water and cow dung. Then the mother and dhai take bath. The mother takes bath with the mixture of turmeric and oil. She puts on new saree. After that the woman can touch every body. Then the woman is given a solution of urine of cow and raw milk by their priest (Nayak); to sprinkle it every where and over her body. The woman takes it and mixes this with her hair. Then she bathes her child with the urine of cow and unboiled milk.

After doing all these rituals, the woman can sleep with her mother-in-law. But after one month she is allowed to cook and to sleep with her husband. But for these days she sleeps with her mother-in-law.

On 21st day (Name giving ceremony): On the 21st day they arrange a 'yagyan' or holy fire. All the members can take any thing but except sour food within these period. Brahmin (Akhaya Joshi), performs this yagyan. They do yagyan with 'nabani woods'. After the completion of yagyan the priest prepares 'panchamruta' with ghee, jaggery, curd, honey and milk. Then they give this 'panchamruta' to all the family members and relatives. Then they make 'liya' out of grain and distribute it among all people who are present in this ceremony. On that day the Banjara people give name to the child, after which they ring a bell. The child's father-sister (Nana) gives the name to child. Both the relatives of mother's side and father's side are present in this ceremony. In this ceremony, the maternal uncle and aunt bring sweets, dress and gold ornaments for the mother and child.

After completion of yagyan they worship and pray to their ancestral deity by giving some offerings. At the time of name giving, both mother and child wear new dress.

After the name giving ceremony is over the male and female members of the village, their relatives and the Brahman bless the child by throwing rice over the child. Then the family members arrange a feast for all the members and villagers.

After 6 months: Upto 6 months the child is given mother's milk. But when they feel the mother's food is not sufficient for the child, they grind rice and boil it in water. With it they mix jaggery or sugar and form a thick liquid food which they give to the child. After that the child starts to sit slowly and gradually.

After 1 year: When the child becomes one-year-old, they

feed the baby boiled wheat and jaggery. Usually they spread boiled wheat and jaggary on a new cloth. After that all family members sit on the cloth and feed the mixture to the baby and help the baby for walking. They also celebrate on this day.

Banjara people have a strong belief in the effects of evil eyes. So to protect the baby, they put a black thread 'kaliasar' around the neck of the baby. They also take salt, chilli, two mustards and move it in front of the child from face to foot of the baby and throw it into the hearth. Then they twist the fingers and never look back. They believe, if the chili gives a smell then the baby is not affected by evil eyes. If the chili does not give any smell, then it means the baby is affected by evil eyes. They hang a coconut in front of house to protect the baby and house from the evil eyes.

Rukmani has a child of six months. She observes all the restriction of pregnancy period. She took only rice, dal, and potato twice in a day. She did not eat non-vegetaian food. She was restricted to wear black bangles and brush her teeth with sand during pregnancy periods.

PUBERTY

In spite of the advent of modernization, Banjara people still love as well as maintain their cultural tradition. In Banjara society there is a lot of restriction for girls.

Usually, there is no ceremony for boys, when a boy attains maturity. But in case of the girl, it becomes quite remarkable. With the first coming of menstrual blood, the family members celebrate it. The Banjara knows menstruation as 'Handimar'. The great aim of initiation is to convert a girl into a fruitful married woman. During this puberty stage the Banjara people observe various restrictions. Among Banjara, a girl normally attains maturity at the age of 13 or 14. When the periods first start, at that time the girl first informs it to her friends, who inform it to the girl's mother. After that, they keep the girl for six days in a separate room. If they have no separate room, then they keep the girl at the corner of house where no male members can see her. At that time the mother, her sister and all female members of the house take care of the girl. For six days she does not take bath, remains with the only worn dress and sits at the corner of the house. Her mother or other female members of the village provide her foods. But she is allowed to wash utensils herself. She bathes in the early morning on sixth day. But she does not go alone. She goes with the female members, but she does not see the face of any male.

On 7th day: On the seventh day, the pollution of menstrual period is believed to be over. This day is very important for all of them. Upto six days the girl does not take bath, but on the seventh day she takes bath very early in the morning with many female members. While coming home she does not look back and throws her worn dress into water. She washes her hair, massages turmeric and oil on her body with the help of her sister or other female relatives. On this day, the person who wants to make the girl their daughter-in-law comes to girl's house with clothes and other toiletry things. On these days the girl can not eat non-vegetarian food but all other types of foods she can take. On this day they arrange a feast, in which all villagers are invited and also relatives are invited. But they do not eat non-vegetarian food items. Then they arrange a 'yagyan' (holy fire) to satisfy nine planets, to which they call as 'Grahashanti'.

On this occasion all the people present gifts to the girl like dresses and ornaments. If they do not do this ritual then they have a belief that the person who will marry that girl, will die soon after the marriage.

During puberty period the girl does not touch water. From that day they do not sleep with their mother. If there is full moon night or no moon night in between these seven days of the girl, just after three or five days of pollution, comes out of the house.

The psychology of Banjara people: They think if a girl gets menstruation at night while sleeping on floor, it is very good. But if she gets menstration while sleeping on bed then it is a bad symbol and causes harm to everybody. When it occurs, they say 'Graha-dosha' affects the girl.

Therefore they sacrifice cock, goat and do yagyan. Sorcerer (Gunia) does all these sacrifices. He also sacrifices coconut, parua, chemera bird etc. This initiation ceremony is called as 'Karma' by Banjara. They say if a girl menstruates on Thursday then it is very good sign, they call that girl as Laxmi. The girl who is born on Sunday is also considered special. According to Banjara people if the girl's menstruation occurs on Tuesday then it is called as 'Devidasha'. If there is irregularity in menstruation cycle then they take 108 hibiscus flowers and offer it to Pedrani Devi. Then they again restart their periods.

But this restrictionis different for a woman. When a newly married woman has her pollution period, she does not touch water and the deities and is not allowed to cook food for any person. She remains in a room and she does not share bed with her husband. But when the newly married woman becomes aged, then the woman does not touch the deities, water and does not cook food. She is allowed to sleep with her husband in a same room. But they do not sleep in one bed. The husband sleeps on bed and wife on floor. Women spread mat on floor and sleep on it during this period.

So Banjara equally observes this pollution period as we practice in our society.

MARRIAGE RITUAL

Marriage is a pivotal, universal social institution almost found in each and every society. Different authors give different definition of marriage.

According to **John Beattie**, 'marriage is a union between a man and woman such that the children born are the legitimate off spring of both the partners.'

According to **Majumdar** 'marriage is a socially sanctioned union of male and female or as a secondary institution device by society to sanction the union of the mating of male and female for the purpose of;

a) Establishing a household.
b) Entering into a relation.
c) Procreation.
d) Providing care for the off spring.

According to **Malinowski** "marriage is for procreation and maintenance of children".

According to Rig Veda 'the main aim of marriage is to have hybrid progeny'.

So the term marriage has different meanings. They call it as 'Bihaghar', but Banjara people marry only to increase their family. They have a belief that the people who do not have child, they do not go to heaven. That is the main reason for their marriages.

In Banjara community there is a great restriction upon the girls so they do not allow a girl to have a love marriage. They only practice arranged marriage. I did not find any case of love marriage in their community.

When a girl attains her maturity, on the seventh day, the interested person come with clothes and sweets and asks the hand of the girl. During ancient times, they perfomed the marriage of a girl when she was 12 to 14 years old. But now they marry off the daughters after 16 years. The term they used for asking the girl's hand and accepting it is called as "Mangan". The priests they invited for doing marriages are Hindi Brahmins. Because they believe Oriya Brahmins usually do not know their tradition. They arrange marriage outside their clan. It means they believe in clan exogamy. Banjara people worship to Gurunanak before the bridegroom goes to the bride's house. Male members of the family do it. In this worship they worship Talwar, Dhaal and Turban in the name of Gurunanak at night. They make a ritual diagram of it with rice powder, puta diya in between this, and covered it with rice powder. They put pot to which they worship as symbol of Gurunanak. Above this diagram they put a coin and 'Kathari'. They offer chapatti as prasad. They grind chapatti and mix gud and ghee with it and take this as sacred offal. Male members prepare this sacred offal. But the female members prepare labsif as sacred offal. This Puja starts between 7–8 P.M. After completion of Gurunanak worship, they do 'pitru-puja'. Then they take their lunch and on next morning they get ready for marriage.

They offer labsif in the name of their ancestors. The Nayak (village head man) is their main mediator. He usually goes to bride's house for fixing marriage. He also goes with the bridegroom to bride's house.

At Bride's house: They keep the girl, who is going to marry, in a separate room. After the bridegroom arrives, the girl's side do the 'Bata barana' and present watch or ring. The bridegroom usually comes with his father, other relatives and Nayak of his village. At that time the female members of girl's family open her hair bare and she starts to cry. The brother gives a sandal bindi to his sister. Then the bridegroom and bride both sit and they are separated by screen. Then the bride and bride groom take bath with mahendi, ghee and turmeric, done by other female members of the girl's family. Then they are given a bunch of thread and the bridegroom wears it in the hand. But the bride wears it around the neck.

Marriage Altar: Barber facing towards east prepares marriage altar. Then seven unmarried girls come with water and wash the mandap. Before doing marriage the bride's family also gives 'shradha' (kalpache) to their 'pitrupurusha'. They put two wooden sticks at the two side of mandap. The yagyan or sacrifical fire needs to be in between this. The 'vedi' is in a square form. At each corner three 'kalash' with mango leaf, coconut and nut (gua) are placed.

Then the bridegroom and bride go round from one corner of mandap to another side. Then the priest does the yagyan and then the 'hastha ganthi' takes place. After that the boy and girl live in a room, in which they keep a talwar in between them. They are restricted to go to each other's side and they light 'diya' at night which the unmarried girls are not allowed to see. At night the bridegroom ask the bride for 'anchal' in which she gives sweets and money. Other girls of the bride's family take these things from bride. This room is called as 'madhusala'. Before going to 'madhusala' there is some rituals performed at alter. A cloth is placed in between the bridegroom and bride. At that time the girl's in-laws give sweets in the hand of the boy to put it in the mouth of the girl and also the girl is given sweets to give it to the boy. After that they go to 'madhusala'. In the morning after waking from bed they go for bath. But nobody can see them before bathing. They again go to alter and sit. Then turmeric water is showered first by the girl towards boy and then by bridegroom towards bride. They repeat this process seven times. The Banajra women then give bronze and coins to the boy and girl. These materials are placed in between them. Then both of them try to take it away. The one who takes all these materials, is declared winner. The defeated person has to obey any condition of the winner. Then a feast is given from bride's family. All members of village are also invited. Then the bridegroom and bride are given rice, curd and sweets to eat.

All this occurs only for two days. But in early time the bridegroom stayed at bride's house for six months, and then it gradually decreased to three months, one month, 15 days, 8 or 7 days. But now it is only of 2 days. They also place 'ladan' on a bull which is decorated and send it with the girl as her dowry.

At Bridegroom's house: When the bride with bridegroom reaches her mother-in-law's house, all the members of the boy's family bring ghee, comb, diya and water in front of them and see the face of new bride. Then the female members of the family sprinkle water and ghee on the head of boy and girl for seven times. Then they put a bindi on the forehead of both bridegroom and bride. After that they put 'okhara' (a local term) at the door and both of the boy and girl are told to cross it by jumping. Then the bridegroom and bride sit on a mat. The bride takes a small boy to her 'kola or goad' for four times and the bridegroom takes a small girl to his 'kola or goad' three times. They worship (both boy and girl) to their 'Ista Devi' or 'Ista Deva'. After few days the newly married bride goes to Siva temple for worshipping and does Satyanarayan puja. But when a girl is married, then she can't touch the Goddess of her father's house.

Restrictions

(1) When a bride touches her elder brother-in-law then the brother-in-law will give sweets, coconut to all people.

(2) But when a woman touches her younger sister's husband then the person will give sweets, coconut to all family members. They are free with their mother-in-law.

(3) The girl whose engagement is over and is going to marry is allowed to go to all relatives houses but can't go outside the village.

After the completion of all these rituals the newly married bride holds 'pot' filled with water and a number of brushing stick (datun) in it. It is covered by 'shanna'. She places it on her head and by holding it with hand, she takes the blessing of all in-laws. Then in next day morning she takes the 'pot' and pours the water in it near 'ushributa' tree. This shows a new responsibility upon the newly married bride. In ancient times there prevailed the custom of bride price but now they practice dowry system.

DEATH RITUAL

For Banjara people the concept of death is a very interesting one. They believe in spirit. They have a belief if a person died in middle age or in due to any accident then the spirit of that person does not go away. It is always around them and sometimes cause many harm to them.

Among Banjara when a person dies then all his cousins come to the dead person's house. Then the members of that house eat 'Mitti Bhat' which is cooked by other relatives. Then family members and villagers carry the dead body. They keep salt, ghee, rice and cloth toward the north side of the dead body. While taking the dead body they sprinkle coins and shells on the road. Then, they place the dead body at road side, when they see a berry plant. After that they take the dead body. The head of the dead body is toward north and the other portion is toward south direction. The elder son gives the funeral pyre, and if the person had no son then any member of his family can give the funeral pyre.

Banjara call the dead body as 'murda'. In which they carry the dead body is 'khat'. When they burn the dead body, they do not come back home until the head of that dead person blasts. The dead body is carried by four people and the first two persons change their place with the last two persons. Then after coming back they bath in pond and take the 'mitti bhat'.

For a dead body which is buried in burial ground 'mashan pada', the length of the hole dug is 5.5 to 6 cm, breadth is 1.5 inch and depth is 2 feet. But they told that when they dig a hole for dead body, it also depends on the physical feature of the dead person. If the person is healthy one then they dig a large hole for him but if he or she is a thin person then they dig a small hole for the dead body.

For each and every type of death they perform different types of rituals:

- If a child is died then they take it in on a pot and bury the body behind their houses. They do not take this dead body to burial ground.
- If any Banjara people died because any diseases like small pox, malaria, chicken pox etc., instead of burying it, they throw the dead body into the forest.
- If a married woman died then Banjara women massage turmeric to the dead body, give a new sari to the dead body, give a bindi which is the mixture of vermilion and sandal etc. then they take the dead body to burial ground. Her elder son gives the funeral pyre. If the woman has no son then her husband will give the funeral pyre. Then they take the remains of body after it is cold, mainly after three days.But in our society, the remains are taken after one day.
- When a son dies, then the father gives the funeral pyre. If the father died then his son carries the dead body. The first two men who carry the dead body are his sons and the last two men who carry the dead body are two brothers of the dead man. If the person has no brothers then other members can carry the dead body.

When the funeral pyre is given to the dead body, at that time they give ghee and salt to the dead body, so that the ashes do not fly from fire. Banjara observes this pollution for ten days. On eleventh day they purify themselves.

On 3rd day they clean the house, clothes and wash the house with cow dung water. The washer-man cleans the clothes. The Barber cuts their nail and all members shave their hair. But female members only cut their nails. All the family members including other relatives make turban of a cloth for the elder son of the family. The relatives bring clothes. Then they give a white cloth to the elder son of the family. The cloth is brought by the relatives. Then they give a white cloth to the widow. Then the cousin looks non-vegetarian food for all members of the house. All members eat that food, except the unmarried girl. The relatives are from another village. In the same village the same clan people are invited for cooking 'mitti bhat'. Then they take the ashes of the dead person in a box and placed it inside the soil above which a water pot is hung on a tree and the water drops fall on it. This is done by the male members of the family. The female members light diya in front of the ashes both morning and evening.

This diya is lighted up to ten days. There is no fixed limitation of burying these ashes. They keep these ashes for 5 or 6 years. But when they want or when they have sufficient money, they float it in Ganga river. They put the ashes like this for the cool of the body remains.

After three days the Banjara people put water and rice powder on the place where the person died. It occurs at night. Then a symbol is formed on rice powder automatically. Then at that place they put a photograph of the dead person and worship it.

On this day they also invite their 'makara', who also bring clothes, sweets and rice with him. Then they cook separately for their 'makara' and also eat the cooked food within their family. They call it as 'mahaprasad'. The cousins are invited. They come and cook food for all. Then they again come on 10th day.

Only from the evening of third day they are semi-purified. They can touch everything from the evening of third day. But before that day they do not touch anything.

On tenth day they eat sweets in the name of the dead person and they believe the soul of the dead person will leave from the body remains that are kept inside the soil. On the 10th day they kill goat and sheep. Then arrange a grand feast for the villagers and cousins. With these non-vegetarian foods, sweets, cakes, labsif are also given to the villagers and to their cousin. They arrange plays and 'Daskathia' for entertainment, only when an old person has died.

On the eleventh day they arrange yagyan for the peace of the soul of dead person. They have a belief that if there is any type of fault in the soul, then by doing yagyan all this will be excused.

The Banjara people call this fault as –

(1) "Ekpa dosha" One foot.

(2) "Duipa dosha" Two foot.

During Dussehra they also give 'pitrusarat'. It is meant for the maintenance of house and peace of the dead ancestors. They invite all the Brahmins. The Brahmins do worship in the name of their dead ancestor. They give curd, honey, fish, rice, potato, to the Brahmin which they call as 'Dakshina'. Then the elder son's wife cooks labsif and puts five times into hearth in the name of the dead persons and gives five times water in to the hearth for washing the hands of their dead ancestors. They have a belief that the materials given by them to Brahmins are eaten by their ancestors in heaven.

They have a belief that only married person's dead body is burnt. But the dead body of unmarried person is dug in the grave yard. If they get maximum woods then they burn it, if they do not get maximum woods then they bury the dead body.

In ancient time, they burnt the ornaments, and materials with dead body. When an unmarried girl died, they buried the ornaments and the daily use dresses of the girl with the dead body. The ladies are not allowed to the grave yard or to perform any burial ritual at the burial ground.

6

RELIGIOUS FUNCTIONARIES

INTRODUCTION

A religious specialist or functionary is one who devotes himself to a particular branch of religion or is viewed organizationally, as a major part of a religious system. In societies or contexts where such religious power is regarded as an impersonal, anthropologist describe it as magic and to those who manipulate the power as magicians.

The religious practitioners or functionaries gain certain advantages from their relationship to the sacred, such as prestige, power and goods. These religious functionaries are the mediators between God and people.

In Banjara society there are various religious specialists are found. These are priest (pujari) sorcerer, (gunia-magical specialist), Diviner (Bhagat), family head and village head man (Nayak) etc. These specialists interact differently with different types of God. To different deities they (specialists) offer coconut, different types of flowers and animal sacrifice for the deity's satisfaction. They do this only to maintain a peaceful life, get cured of various diseases and to avoid various unfortunate events.

RELIGIOUS SPECIALISTS

Priest (Pujari)

According to Max Weber, the critical feature of priesthood is that "specialization of a particular group of person in the continuous operation of acult like enterprise, permanently associated with particular norms, places and times as related to specific social group."

Lessa and Vogt expand these differences: a Shaman's powers come by 'divine stroke', a priest's power is inherited or is derived from the body of codified and standardized ritual knowledge that he learns from older priest and later transmits to successors (Lessa and Vogt, 1958-1965: 410).

The priest is usually considered as a specialized person who has direct access to supernatural entities. Between the priest and the deity intervenes the institution. Priests may therefore be classified as institutional functionaries in the religious domain. The priestis concerned with the conservation and maintenance of a deposit of beliefs and practices handed down as a sacred trust from the founders of the social or religious system.

Priests are found mainly in food gathering and agricultural societies. Banajra people are agriculturalists and they do have priests for all sorts of ritual performances. Banjara people call the priest as 'pujari'. The datas are from two different villages namely Dabriguda and Hanspada. In Dabriguda village the 'pujari' is of Gond tribe and in Hanspada village the pujari is of Ghasi caste, mainly schedule caste people. He performs all the ritual performances of the village deities who are revered by all people irrespective ofcaste and tribe. He fixes the date of any festivals and does all the religious sacrifices. Banjara people give a great respect to the priest. For the worship of Banjara deities, they do not invite the Priest. But only for the worship of deities, which are influenced by Hindu culture, they invite the Priest. They invite the priest to worship the Basterein, Thakurani, Barsarmajhi, Daragadhiani, Bhandarsuni, Badamaili and Sanamail Goddess. All these are village level deities. So both the Banjara and other tribe/caste people combinely worship these deities. Barsarmajhi is the priest of Basterein.

In all these deities worship, the priest plays the main role and does not take any food till after the completion of the worship. The priest takes food. But he does not take non-vegetarian food. He wears dhoti at the time of worshipping. He does not allow any body to the 'Devataghar' at the time of worshipping. He restricts especially women. He alone does all the work of deities. He cleans all the materials of Gods and then worships them. He follows all the rituals and while worshipping he does not talk with anybody. At the time of pollution period, mainly during the birth of child or death of any person, he does not allow the members of that familyto enter into 'Devataghar' and participate in the worship. While worshipping, he does all sacrifices. He does the sacrifice of sheep, cock, goat, pig, pigeon etc.

Only in one or two occasions they invite Brahmin priest. In the worship of Kali Devi, Trinath mela and in marriage ceremony they invite or call Oriya Brahmin priest. The priest who worships in Balijatara festival, is called Bhukia. The name of 'Bhukia' is Judhistira Nayak. The 'Bhukia' may be of their own caste.

They practice various rituals and also lead an orderly and lawful life. Therefore there are various rules regarding the appointment of the post of priest. The post of priest (pujari) is hereditary and only elder son has the right to become the priest. It occurs only after the death of priest. If the pujari has no children, then they bring another pujari from another village. This occurs for temporary period. But after that in a communal meeting they again select new priest. Goddess is more powerful.

The priest, while worshipping never sit in front of Goddess. They always sit at oneside of Goddess. Because they think the Goddess is none powerful than them, so it is a kind of respect to the deity.

Village Headman (Nayak)

Without a headman a village can not exist. In Banjara society they call their village headman as 'Nayak'. Banjara people also invite 'Nayak' for worship of various other deities. Nayak worships the Banjari Devi, Swargamaili, Danteswari, Matrala, Lukudia, Ashawari etc. While worshipping to these deities he follows all the rules and restriction. He does not eat any food and only after worshipping he can take any food, but this must be veg food. He also does all the sacrifices to deities. He does not allow women to see the puja. In some cases he also takes the help of elder person of family.

Besides these religious acts she also performs all other activities. In every activity 'Nayak' takes the help of medicine man and elder person of village. The 'Nayak' of Hanspada village is Kumar Naik. If any crime is done by any person, then the 'Nayak' and all his other members of village fine him to give Rs. 101 or Rs. 1001. But it is charged, taking in account of the financial condition of the person.

If a girl goes away with a boy, then the family of the

girl has to pay a fine of Rs. 101. They give a 'mana' fine for it. When the girl comes back to her home, she again pays 'mana' fine and gives a feast to all members of village. This work is controlled by 'Nayak'. In various economic activities people also consult the 'Nayak'. Nayak has main role in various ceremonies at the time of initiation, marriage, funeral rites. After taking permission of 'Nayak' and the completion of religious activities, the people start to celebrate their ceremonies.

The post of 'Nayak' is hereditary in nature. After the death of 'Nayak' or when the 'Nayak' is unfit to carry out all works, then the leadership is transferred to his elder son. But if the elder son is unable to hold this post, then it is held by next son of the 'Nayak'. The Banjara people have no desire for 'Nayak' post. Therefore it is hereditary and they respect 'Nayak'.

In very recent time, Banjara people moved from one place to another place in a group. After that they decided to choose a leader by seeing his extraordinary qualities. They wanted that the leader should control their group. They called this leader as 'Nayak'. From that day the Banjara people continue their customs.

Medicine man (Baida)

In Hanspada village the medicine man is Jogi Naik. They call him as 'Baida'. He assists the 'Nayak' in some of religious cases. In Hanspada village the medicine man is the brother of 'Nayak'. The medicine man collects various herbs. Then he prepares medicine. Before giving medicine to people he first worships in the name of Siva and their 'Ista devi – Taljabhabani', and then he gives various medicines. His post is hereditary. The villager respect him and give him dhoti, towel, rice and sweets, when he goes to any house in any occasion or festival. He played a dual role in their society as practitioner as well as farmer as he is also involved in various seasonal economic activities.

Family Headman

Among Banjara, family headman also has some religious functions. The rituals or ceremonies or worshipping to various deities, which occur in the family level, are controlled by family headman or elder person of family. Mainly, the worship of Taljabhabani, Taljakankali, Dula, Pir, Pedrani Devi, is done by elder members of family. He also does all sacrifices and cleaning of deity's accessories. While doing puja, he does not talk to anybody, does not eat anything. Only after doing worship, he eats the sacred offal of the worship.

MAGICAL SPECIALISTS

The Sorcerer (Gunia or Guru)

Like various religious specialists among Banjara, various magical specialists are also found and from various magical specialists 'Gunia' is one. The patient or victim has belief in the power of 'Gunia'. The Gunia's belief lies in the effectiveness of his techniques. Finally the faith and expectations of the group, which constantly act as a sort of gravitational field within which the relationship between 'Gunia' or be witched is located and defined. These are the main criteria, which are to be required within 'Gunia', then only he can be success in his work.

The 'Gunia' learns magic from his 'Guru'. The Banjara

people also called 'Gunia' as 'Guru'. When the 'Gunia' utilizes his magic for helping everybody then it is called as white magic. But when the magic is practiced to harm anybody then it is called as black magic.

The sorcerer or 'Gunia' maintains an intimate relationship with the spiritual world or with the forces of the super natural. He also advises people how to deal with illness and cases of misfortune. The Guru has a special role in society. Everybody respects him. In every festivals or such occasions they invite 'Gunia' and treat him very carefully. In marriage the 'Shanna' place over pot is only taken out by 'Gunia'.

Role and Post: When a person is constantly affected by any disease, then he first goes to the 'Guru' or 'Gunia'. Gunia first takes 'rashi oil' and put two to three drops of urine of the person in it. Then the 'Gunia' can see the evil eyes or disease from which the person is suffering. The 'Gunia' advises the person to satisfy some deities or to take some herbal medicine. After that the person gets cured. Guru also controls the bad activities of witch and her bad magic practices.

When any spirit is affected to any person then that person will go to the 'Gunia'. Then the 'Gunia' first reads some mantras. He sprinkles water in the space, where he makes the ritual diagram for spirit. No body touch the water. If dog, cat touches the water then it is polluted, only 'Gunia' can bring the water. Then the affected person sits in front of the ritual diagram and the guru sits in front of affected person facing towards west and sprinkles water over that man by uttering some sacred spells. Then the spirit which has possessed the victim is automatically controlled by 'Gunia'.

When any person is affected by Dokra bhut, Tengua bhut, Chirangul, then the person goes to 'Gunia'. When any person is affected by God and Goddess and that person is always suffering from disease like body-ache, blood dysentery etc. Then the person goes to the 'Gunia' to know the cause of disease. The 'Gunia' by his power finds the causes and advices the person to sacrifice some animals in the name of the deities because of which all these unfortunate has happened.

I have collected data from Chandrabhanu Naik who also suffered from various diseases and the 'Gunia' advised him to sacrifice something in the name Goddess. Now he is cured and in fine health.

When any new child is born, then the parents of the child go to the 'Gunia'. The 'Gunia' gives them a 'Tabij' to protect their child from any evil eyes. When a girl is first initiated and if she has some fault then it is called as 'Devi dosha'. The 'Guru' will tell this and advise the parents of the girl to sacrifice cock, coconut, chenera, paura etc. When the 'Pisacha' does not go away from a person, then the 'Guru' takes the person to the graveyard and pricks 5 to7 nails on a tree and tries to capture the 'Pisacha' in that tree. If the 'Gunia' can't cure a person then with the help of 'majurmutha' they tell spirit to go out of body. If the spirit still does not leave, then the Banjara people take pigeon, lemon, flowers, bangles, vermilions, cajole and put it in water and go around it seven times. Then the spirit goes round in that place. Dasharati Naik is the main 'Guru' or 'Gunia', who knows every sacred spell. Only the males are 'Gunia'. He is very decent in nature and a great devotee of God. He is very silent in nature. He does not eat at anybody's house.

Anybody can learn the sacred spell and utilize it for the well being of people. He is the main Guru, from whom many other people learn sacred spell. Sadhumajhi is another 'Gunia' in the village.

The Diviner (Bhagat)

The diviner is also another magic specialist. Banjara people call diviner as 'Bhagat'. The diviner is a diagnostician who diagnoses the disease and solves various problems of people. Divination is enquiry about future events or matter. It is mainly found in preliterate societies.

Banjara people believe it is the wish of the deities to whom the deities are transmigrated. Banjara people told that only Goddesses are transmigrated. Gods are never transmigrated to any person. Mainly Pedrani Devi and Thakurani are transmigrated to person. But that person must live in a very principle manner. The person must be great devotee of Goddess. They said every Goddess has 'shira' and priest. They called this process as 'Devikheliba'.

Role and Post: At the time of worshipping of 'Pedrani Devi', they ring a bell at the end of puja. At that time the person will automatically come. He then turns around and sits down. The person wears a dhoti and ties a towel around his waist; the person takes vermilion from Devi Pedrani and puts a mark on his forehead. After that Devi is transmigrated to that person. Then the air of 'Dhuna' is given to his face by which Devi becomes cooled down. After that various village members ask different questions regarding their family problem, disease, educational problem. The 'Bhagat' will answer everything and give various solutions to various problems. The 'Bhagat' by seeing the face of person can himself know why the person has come here.

The name of one 'Bhagat' is Padma Naik. A 'Bhagat' may be male or female one. Pedrani Devi transmigrated to Padma Naik. The post of 'Bhagat' is not hereditary. 'Bhagat' looks like a simple man or woman. But when Devi is transmigrated they have extraordinary power.

Thakurani is also transmigrated to a male or female person. Thakurani has a dress. The person automatically comes and wears this dress, wears payal. Then that person first sit on a 'Doli' full with nails. Then that person pricks her/his stomach by 'Barcha'. Then that person starts to dance. That person can dance for half to one hour. Then automatically he/she sits on the ground and answers everybody's question.

So the 'Bhagat' has a great role in Banjara society.

Witch (Dakan)

Both witch and Sorcerer learn the same sacred spells. But the Witch uses it for bad purpose or to harm various people. If any person is suffering from disease, poverty and sorrow, then they go to their 'Guru or Gunia'.

The Guru tells them that they are affected by witch and to find out who is the witch among them, the Guru does some anti-magic so that the witch suffers from dysentery or any other disease. Then all people know which person is a witch and was practicing witchcraft. Witch is always a female person in Banjara society.

Features - Banjara people call witch as 'Dakan'. As they say 'Dakan is a normal woman. But they have a tendency to always wear a red Saree and keep the hair open. As the people say, she has comparatively very large eyes. She eats raw meat. However, no body can recognise a witch just by physical visualisation on normal occasions. But an unseen fear will automatically rise in between them. At midnight the 'Dakan' reads and spells (mantra) in the burial/cremation ground in full naked body.

Role - As believed by the 'Dakan', any person who looks at any beautiful lady or gents, they are expected to have evil eye and suffer from some disease. Their evil eyes converts the milk of cow to blood, it also causes the disease of cows, bull, dysentery, blood vomiting of individuals, etc. Due to the black magic, vegetables also do not grow. Then all people inform the happenings to Guru. The 'Gunia' then can know the 'Dakan' and tie her with bamboo sticks then give fire to the bamboo stick. Then the Dakan is dead.

Practice - When an unmarried girl dies, the people bury the dead body of the girl. Then at night the 'Dakan' lights four lamps (diyas) around it and lights threads on fire around the dead body. Then she gives life to the dead body and instructs her to do harm too many people.

In Hanspada and Dabriguda village, there is a lady named 'Sushila', who is believed to practise 'Devi Aradhana' to do harm too many people, who gives diseases and dries trees etc. All people at last knew it and tried to remove her from their village.

But gradually they (mostly the literate) lost belief in witchcraft. In spite of that, it still exists in their society.

MAGIC

Religion and Magic are very closely related. Frazer says that religion and magic are two ways to overcome crisis. Magic is used only for goals. Magic is least potentially directed against the society, and a major accepted group within it or a respected individual in good rapport with the Gods. There are mainly two different types of magic: White Magic and Black Magic. White Magic is practiced by 'Gunia' and Black Magic is practiced by 'Dakan'. Among Banjaras, there is practitioner of white and black magic.

Contagious Magic

Contagious Magic is based on principle of 'once in contact is always in contact'. It is practiced by witch. In Banjara society the witch takes the hair, sand of foot and parts of nails and does 'Mantras' to the individual, due to which they suffers from various diseases. Then the person goes to 'Gunia' .The Sorcerer utters some sacred spells and it is automatically gets cured.

The yellow saree which they wear at the time of marriage, the witch takes some parts of the saree and does some spell (mantra) to it. By which the newly married women does not do any work and always becomes ill. Then the 'Gunia' utters sacred spells and sacrifices cocks. If Devi migrated then it will cure or if any magic is done it will cancel automatically.

Imitative Magic

It is based on principle of 'like produces like'. Banjara people also believe in this magic. The witch forms a doll or 'Kushkhan' of a person to whom she wants to do harm. Then she does to the doll whatever harm she desires to do that person. After that the person starts suffering. Then only sorcerer can control this magic. Sorcerer forms a doll and does according to the witch and sacrifices goat, sheep and rice in front of the doll and offers water to the doll. Then the magic is cancelled.

These are the various magical practices found in Banjara society. In Banjara society the sorcerer (Gunia) has a great role in controlling all the black magic practices.

7

RELIGION AND WORLDVIEW

"Religion and Worldview, Religion is nothing else but Love to God and Man" – *William Penn*

DEFINITION

Worldview reflects how the people comprehend the life situation, and with what mindset they do so. Therefore worldview is the expression of totality of experience. Worldview describes the whole reality, secular and sacred, physical and supernatural. The worldview of a culture is the basic outlook of most of the members of a society.

Worldview attains especially, the way the world looks to people looking out and the way a man looking at a particular society and himself in relation to all else sees himself. It is the properties of existence as distinguished from and related to the self. Worldview is the most conflicted and cognitive concept in reference to observable things. Worldview is the way to characterize universal human nature.

Worldview provides order for human existence, like religion, magic, myth, ritual etc. Every society provides deity by which it reflects the worldview of the society. Individuals in which they propitiate are their worldview. Supernatural world is just an extension of social reality for projection of society. It is not merely a philosophical by product of each culture.

Clyde Kluckhohn and Leighton (1949) discuss the Navaho way of life and state that apart from ethics and values the Navaho also have certain 'basic conviction' regarding life and enumerate these in term of basic premises and formulae. The Navaho assumptions about life are generally unsaid, but no characteristic Navaho doing or saying makes senses unless it is related to Navaho conviction about life.

Mendel Baum (1955a) lists three types of relationship to distinguish the contents of worldview: man to man, man to nature and man to supernatural relationship.

Forde (1954) in his introduction to African worlds maintains that worldview is expressed not only in the belief system but is also derivable from customs, rituals and actions. There is a close relationship between beliefs and the context in, which they arise.

Alan Dundes states folklore as the most important source for study of worldview.

The overview of the definition of worldview clearly indicates relationship between social structure and worldview. Worldview constitutes ethos, themes, cultural emphasis etc. which do not influence the direction of life styles of a people holding such worldview. Worldview must be that which by its existence influences the lifepattern. (S.C. Dube, 1977:61)

Bose states that the worldview of a community does not remain constant but is reshaped as its components keep changing.

Ghosh (1968) quotes, Maquet to the effect that the worldview of a society is based on experiences both past and present of the group. According to him 'worldview is a mental disposition or a way of looking at things'. It is transmitted from one generation to other and is conditioned by culture, language and religion.

Soltax (1941) in a seminar paper 'worldview and social relation in Guatmala'. Soltax distinguished worldview from social relation. He suggested that perception of the social relation enters into the 'mental apprehension of reality' i.e. Worldview – Soltax observed that Guatmalan Indian who do not acculturate to each others, continue to have a primitive worldview, although they appear to have had a 'civilized' type of impersonal market oriented system of socio-economic relation since Precambrian time.

Surjit Sinha (1957a) on the paper, the tribal culture of peninsular India suggests the ideological system of the tribal covers man to supernatural, man to nature and man to man relationship. God is classified as benevolent and malevolent. These Gods are portrayed, as being more interested in personal loyalty than in any demonstration of ethical or moral virtues. Ritual is performed mainly to avoid sickness and death. There is belief in existence of soul after death. They have no idea about heaven, hell, no reward, no punishment for good or bad deeds after death.

There is some sort of belief in reincarnation. Man-nature relationship belief shows natural universe to be continuous with the human world of interaction and sentiments. Man, nature and supernatural are all bound within a common boundary of relationship. The entire universe is believed to be animated by spiritual being. The man-man relationship is confined to their tribal world. Elders are respected, children are valued and bareness is feared. Males dominate social life. They emphasize on pleasure and on maintenance of reciprocal and obligatory relationship. There is little desire to achieve high status and the aspiration levels in terms of material achievement are low.

NATURALISTIC WORLDVIEW

Naturalism is the environment approach, which achieves adjustment by altering some apart of the environment itself so as to change interaction between the material factors, which produce phenomena. Every society no matter how 'primitive' has a body of naturalistic customs by which it adjusts to its environment. The customs, which form society's naturalist theory, are science while customary naturalistic practices are its technology (J.S. Slotkin, 1950: 1561).

(A) The Banjara Universe

The Banjara people's idea of Universe is very different from the modern scientific theories. They have no idea about the real size of earth. They divide their whole universe into three parts: the sky or 'Sarag', the earth or 'marta' and under the ground or "patala". They have a belief that after the death, the good and noble souls go to 'sarag' and evil souls go to 'patala' or Narak.

They told - 'Indra' is the king of all God and Goddess. He lives in sky. With Indra all other Goddess are also there. They believe in sky there are many stars, clouds, sun or 'Dharama Devta', moon etc. They believe on earth, different types of plants, trees, insects, men, cocks, goats, air, well or (era), dam or (munda), are present.They said those who have life are mainly present on earth. They are mainly uneducated people. So the Banjara people know that under the ground different types of metals, minerals, water are stored. They believe that in ancient times, Bhagaban Vishnu stayed under the ground and the snake holding him is also there.

Banjara people believe that the whole world or universe is controlled by Vishnu and Shiva. So they call them as 'Bhagaban'. The Banjara people think, when the supernatural deities are dissatisfied with the people living in the world, then they send thunder and storm to this world. They say the Goddesses are more temperamental than Gods. So the Goddess do more harm to people and need animal sacrifices to cool down.

(B) Concept of Time

The Banjara people also determine their time with the help of the Sun and the Moon. They divide the whole year into twelve months and calculate the months with the help of the full moon and the new moon. Among Banjara, the young poeple are more conscious about time than the old ones. Young people are more conscious about their future, which is neglected by the old people.

When the cock crows it is early morning and when sunrises in the sky, they think it is morning or 'Suba'. Then they go to their work or 'Karma'. When they feel slight heat, they think it is 8 A.M. When they feel more heat or when they feel hungry it is 12 to 1 P.M. When they feel less heat then it may be 3 or 4 P.M. They think if the pigeon sounds three times in night then it is midnight or if they see stars forming a shape of plugging machine, it may be also midnight.

But now every house, the people have watch. They do all their activities by seeing the clock. Old people are not able to see the time in watch. Mostly younger generation people are using this watch.

(C) Counting and Measurement

The Banjara people measure their rice by 'Gida', 'Sola', 'Orda' and 'Mana'. They measure their land with a traditional stick.

(D) Knowledge of Ecology

Ecology is the interaction of environment with living beings. The Banjara people are closely related to their environment. They never exploit their nature. They mostly depend upon forests. They collect various food materials and animals from forest. They also worship their mountains for rain and for their protection. They category their animals mainly as edible and non-edible. Animals are sacrificed in the name of deities. The animals are mainly male animals. These animals are goat (Bakra), sheep (gadra), cock (kukudi), swan (hansa) etc. The non-edible animals are mainly residing inside the deep forest. They want to kill the tiger (janwar), because if they won't kill the tiger then the tiger will kill them. If snake bites anybody, then the person will die. It is also a non-edible animal.

There are different types of trees around them. They believe trees help them very much. Mainly saltree (saragi) and piasal tree (Bija) are very important for them. They believe some trees also have poisonous fruits, by eating which anyone can be harmed.

(E) Occupational Categories

Banjara people are mainly agriculturalists. In every season they cultivate different types of crops. Besides this most of the people have cows, bulls, goats etc. By selling milk of cows they earn money. Bulls are mainly used for agriculture purpose.

But due to impact of urbanization, most of the Banjara people started to go to schools and colleges and also wanted to do government jobs. They younger generation people are mainly interested in this and also in politics. But they do not take any interest in agriculture.

But due to impact of industrialization and urbanization, they are also well acquainted with the modern instrument of ploughing, and utilize various modern technologies in agriculture.

(F) Knowledge of Society

The Banjara people divide themselves on the basis of their clan or 'Gotra'. They believe in clan exogamy. They are matrilineal societies. They believe the Laudia clan is superior to other clans. The different clans are laudia, kelut, pamar, ortia, jharabal, etc.

They said that after cutting their crops they become tension free. They give very much respect to their parents and Nayak (village head man). The family head mainly controls the affairs of family. All members take part in cultivation. The old men always think they die and go to 'Swarga'. If some people want help, then the elder sons of village people help them. If someone does not marry or any problem arises in anyone's marriage, then the old people help them and solve their problem. If any girl has unusual relation with any boy then the old people give punishment to the girl and boy.

Banjara people give respect to religious specialists and

intelligent people. They think women should be under the control of men. They do not allow their wife to go anywhere. They always go with their female members. Many times they do not allow ladies to go to their father's house.

In Banjara society older persons always give advice to younger generation. The sons are not allowed to do any work without the permission their father. The older members advise to the younger generation not to do bad works or not to comment on any girls.

(G) Ceremonial Friendship

The Banjara people are not confined only to their own tribe. They also establish relation with other castes or tribes. People also do 'Makara' and 'Gajamung' a type of ceremonial friendship. But this friendship is restricted within the same sex group. It means a boy can make friends only with a boy and girls can make friends only with a girl. These friends are also invited in their birth, marriage and death ceremonies.

Though some Banjaras who are literate are not very traditional in nature, the majority in the society are very much conscious about their natural environment, customs and traditions.

SUPERNATURALISTIC WORLDVIEW

Supernaturalism is the environmental approach, which achieves adjustment by the use of symbols, which stand for immaterial power.

Banjara people worship different types of deities and spirits. So to satisfy them the Banjara people sacrifice animals. The Banjara people have a great faith in their ancestral spirits and various malevolent spirits. Before the observances of any ritual they first worship in the name of their ancestral spirits and then start any ritual works.

(A) Idea of Vice and Virtue

Banjara people call vice as 'pap' and virtue as 'Dharma'. The sorcerer and priest are mediators between the natural and supernatural world. They first take rice by doing yoga or 'jog-sadhna' and offer some of rice in the name of deities. This rice is given to Banjara people by the religious specialist to free them from 'pap'.

They believe in rebirth. If any person does good deeds then he/she will take birth in a good family. If a person does good deeds, then in the next birth that person will again in the human form. If the person does some bad deed, that person in next birth will be a bull or cow. If the person does very bad deeds, then the person will be in the next birth a cock or pig. They think that helping one another, treating guest in a very good manner, taking care of cow, bull and an ailling patient are the 'Dharma' works.

But killing cow, showing misbehavior to parents, showing misbehavior to father and mother-in-laws, doing theft, beating up wife, are the 'pap' works. When they do vice then to be get rid of it, went to Nrusinganath and Puri temple. Then they worship there for atonement. They also give a feast, in which all village people are invited.

(B) Concept of Deities

They believe, when they take any stone, wash it and put a vermilion mark on it, then it is seen as an idol or deity to them. According to them vermilion is the symbol of purity. So the married women always put vermilion on their forehead.

They say there is no sacred spell for Goddess. Sacred spell sare uttered only in the worship of God. The Gods do not want any sacrifice, only Goddesses want sacrifice. They say (Khaa...) at the time of offering sacrifice to deities. They believe, the Goddess who are very much sensitive mainly Pedrani Devi or Thakurani. When they beat drum in front of that type of Goddess, a sound is heard from their sitting place. That sound is – Jannan Jannan...

But in the worship of Dula and Pir, the other families are not allowed even if to see the Puja. With the sacrificed animals in front of different deities they arrange a feast, in which all members of village are invited. Every year they arrange one or two feasts. But in marriage party both boys and girls are invited. But the boys and girls or male and female members in any feast or ceremony are strictly restricted to eat together. The house level deities or clan deities are worshipped for welfare of family or clan members. The village level deities are worshipped of welfare of village people.

They consider Monday, Sunday is good for the worship of the God. But Tuesday and Saturday is preferred for the worship of the Goddess. For marriage Wednesday and Monday are preferred. They think Wednesday and Sunday are very good for agriculture and for every work. Therefore they called it as 'Siddhi Bara'. But Saturday is very bad for starting of any new work.

The younger generation learns the ways of worship from the elder persons. In early times they were interested to learn tricks from sorcerer. But now they are not interested.

They pray to deities for different purposes mainly the male person prays for wealth, child, disease free and happy life, and more success in life. The females or girls pray for good life, success in studies, sons, more wealth, etc. They think all Goddesses are more powerful than Gods.

The people who have sacred knowledge are treated in a better way than the person who has magical knowledge. Mainly the worship which occurs at village level. In that all Banjara people gather, for sacred purpose, only once in a year. A feast is arranged. But for secular purpose, the feasts are arranged for two to three times. Only males are allowed to participate in the feast arranged for sacred purpose. But both males and females are allowed in the feast arranged for secular purpose.

Banjara people give very much respect to their priest. The priest does not go to the house of any lower caste people. He does not take meat of cow and pig. If he does any of the work given above and then does the worship of Goddess then the Goddess become aggressive. The most aggressive Goddess is Pedrani Devi and then Danteswari. The priest also does not take water from any house. He can eat only in the Banjara family. They think Dama, Pana and Muslims are very low caste people. The priest is restricted to go to the houses of these caste people.

They think if they drink water from these lower caste, then it is not so much bad. But if they eat the cooked food at the houses of lower caste people then it is a great sin and they become polluted. Then to be free from pollution they go to the priest. The respect for priest is always constant in their societies.

The Banjara people also maintain good relation with their sorcerer or gunia. In a year they go to 'Gunia' for five to six times. But on other days they do not go to Gunia's house. But in any special occasion they invite the 'gunia' and give respect to him. Besides these when the 'gunia' wishes, he can come to anyone's house. The Gunia can control any malevolent spirits like Chirangal, Pisacha etc.

But the Banjara people hate witch or 'Dakan' very much. If they identify any person to be a witch then they kill that person. They give a great respect to 'Bhagat' or diviner. The Banjara people form many rules and regulations to maintain their society in a decent way or in a perfect order. The Nayak or village headman is also a religious specialist. His function is multi functional. He controls political, economic, and religious activities. The Banjara people show a great respect to Nayak. The position of Nayak and priest or 'Pujari' has equal status in Banjara society. Next to them they give respect to 'Gunia' and then they give respect Diviner or 'Bhagat'.

But with the impact of industrialization, urbanization and modernization some of the worldview of Banjara people has now started to change.

8

CHANGING SCENE

> There is little reason between our actions, which are perpetually changing and fixed and unchangeable laws.
>
> –Montaigne

INTRODUCTION

Change is a universal factor in any society. Life is changing at each and every moment. Changes occur due to changes in natural factors or changes in cultural factors. The religions of Banjara people have undergone some changes due to the impact of education, modernization and local Oriya culture.

Starting with these changes and analyzing changes in an unbreakable truth while we enter into the life, culture and occupation of Banjara people. We must not ignore that fact may be negotiable but the external and internal changing factors are also working there.

When we go through a deep study about the religious structure of Banjara people, we can analyse the factors, which undergo changes. But as they are very traditional minded people so inspite of various changes, the core aspect of religious structure is almost always maintained. Among Banjara people it is found that changes are mainly due to impact of education and Hindu culture.

IDEA ABOUT GODS AND SPRITS

The Banjara people worship different types of deities. Besides Banjara deities they also worship various other deities popular among the local caste people. Due to prolonged habitation within the local Oriya Hindu groups, they have a number of culture contact in day today life as a result of which, now they are fascinated towards some non-Banjara deities propitiated in village by local Oriya Hindus. They worship Hindu deities, like Siva, Laxmi, Trinath, Brundabati and Santoshi Maa in addition to their traditional deities.

In early times, the Banjara worshipped their original deities with devotion or gratitude with lots of fear as well. Because most of their deities are very much aggressive by nature, they had also belief in various spirits. But now due to the influence of modernization and Hindu culture they do not worship their deities with sincerity like before. Now most of them (usually educated ones) also do not have strong belief in any spirit.

The data has also been collected from Dabriguda village for confirmation which reveals some changing situations in Banjara society. A girl named Minakshi, age 21, was observing only Tuesday and Saturday for fasting and worshiping deities. But now due to the impact of the local Oriya culture, she is observing Monday for the propitiation of Lord Siva, Thursday as day of Laxmi Devi and Friday for Santoshi Mata. She fasts on these days and after worshipping these deities, she takes only vegetarian food.

The Banjara worships Lord Siva in the Siva temple on every Monday and on Sivaratri. They worship Laxmi Devi and Santoshi Mata in very ritualistic manner. They also arrange Trinath mela, in which Lord Brahma, Vishnu and Maheswar are worshipped together in a very ritualistic manner. Besides these, they also worship to Kali Maa, Durga Devi during Diwali and Dussehara. For the worship of all these Hindu deities, the Banjara people also invite Brahmin priest. For the worship of there own traditional deities they go to their Banjara priest.

Now, the Banjara people, especially who are literate do not believe so much in the existence of spirits. Though they believe in the existence of ancestral spirits, they do not believe in malevolent spirits like 'Chirangul', 'Pisacha', 'Gadagadia' ghost etc. Due to gradually increasing literacy and impact of various development programmes, the Banjara people have lost their traditional culture slowly and become very much fascinated by modernization. Their beliefs in these evil customs and traditions are also gradually fading.

OBSERVANCES OF FESTIVALS

The Banjara people also observe different Hindu festivals; these festivals are Rakhi-purnima, Holi, Dussehra, Manabasa, Balijatra Nuakhai etc. They learn from the Hindu people their ways of observing these festivals. They accept Hindu priests for the worship or observances of these Hindu festivals.

In ancient times, they were very much restricted to their own culture and to their own festivals. But due to the constant interaction with the Hindus they started to accept some of the Hindu festivals. As per their ancient rituals, they used to observe Holi for three days. On the first day they worshipped HolikaDevi, and played with sand, on second day they played 'phagu' and on the third day they arranged a grand feast in which all villagers participated. But now they observe it only for one day. They worship Holika Devi on morning and play phagu at evening.

Diwali too used to be observed for two days earlier. On first day they did Laxmi Puja and on second day they did Gobardhan Puja. But now they do Laxmi Puja in the morning and Gobardhan Puja in the evening and observe Diwali for just one day.

In early times they followed much more restriction in the observances of Tij festival and Charupuja. But now they are not able to observe these festivals with so much restriction. The local Oriya Hindu festivals such as Dussehra, Manabasa, Balijatra, are observed by Banjara people with a great interest. The Banjara observe these festivals by learning all the procedures of these festivals. Jagara is also observed by the Banjara people in the month of February-March in which the Brahmin priest worships in a ritualistic manner in Siva temple.

Besides these festivals, Banjara people also practice some festivals relating to agriculture. They observe these festivals by coming in contact with the Oriya people. These festivals are Hareliuansh, Pausa Purnima and Nuakhai. In the observances of their own festivals they do not allow any Oriya priest to do the worship. Only their own caste people are allowed to worship their deities and festivals. But now even if in the worship of their own festivals, they to some extent allow the Oriya priest to do Puja.

They also do various ritual friendships like 'Makara' or 'Gajamung'. As the local Oriya people also observe the similar ritual friendship, it is believed that Banjara people might have followed this custom from local Oriya people. They also practise all the rituals that are followed during this friendship. Even they do friendship with non Banjara people and also invite the friend in their all festivals, marriage, death and birth. This is found in case of new generation people and the aged people among them are still very strict and restrictive.

In every society, changes are obvious. But in case of change in Banjara society, only the peripheral aspect of ritual changed at surface and not at the core. Old generation people are still confined to traditional practices about religion and are comparatively more sincere in performing rituals than younger generation people.

OBSERVANCES OF LIFE CYCLE RITUAL

Some changes have also occurred in the practice of birth, marriage, puberty and death. But the older generation people practice these rituals in a more traditional way and in very strict manner. Now most of the younger generation people of Banjara have started going schools and colleges. Most of the people have television and radio. Due to these factors they are more aware about things going on in the world around them and are becoming modern slowly.

In the birth rites as per the ancient norms, the pregnant woman, upto nine month does not take any salty, toxic or acidic foods. She is not allowed to go outside at night. But now the women do not observe any restriction on foods. They take every food. Even they do not believe in any evil spirit. That's why they do not wear any Tabij or obey any restriction relating to evil spirit.

A lady named Rukmani, age 28, is pregnant. She takes every kind of foods in her pregnancy period. She does not believe in any evil spirits, which may cause harm to her baby and herself.

Up to seven days the mother, who is giving birth to new life does not touch anything. She is not allowed to kitchen or 'Devata Ghar' and also barred from sleeping with her husband in a single room. But after seventh day the woman can touch anything only after purifying herself. But she is not allowed to sleep with her husband up to one month and also not allowed to cook food for one month.

But now all these restriction are not followed by the ladies. They can stay with their husbands only after 10 to 15 days. They can also now go to kitchen room after these seven days. But they are not allowed to cook foods for family members.

A lady named Surya Kanti told that they are not allowed to cook foods for family members for one month, she answered that it is only for the reason that they are very weak after delivery. So they do not do any household work, which may give them more strain. That's why they do not cook for one month for their family members.

In case of marriage rituals, they practice various rules and regulation as in our society. In marriage Banjara people first practice bride price system. But now there is no bride price system. Now there is advent of dowry system. They note down the amount of dowry they take from girl's family. So that in any occasion they can give gift of equal amount to their daughter-in-law's house.

The various rituals observed starting from the arrival of bride-groom to the east when both brideg-room and bride go to their own house are now gradually fading. In marriage, at first the bride-groom was staying at bride's house for six months but with the changing time this duration started decreasing. Kanchanbala Naik, age 26, told that she married before four years and in her marriage the bride-groom or her husband Ghanasyama Naik stayed only for two days in her house. This shows the old tradition has continuously started decaying.

In case of initiation of a girl, various customs have changed.When a girl was first matured they kept her in a separate room for six days. But now they keep the girl for only 3 to 5 days. A girl named Tillotoma of Hanspada village narrated, when she first got her maturity, she was kept in a separate room only for five days. On the sixth day she got her purity. On seventh day the old generation Banjara people would usually be arranging a 'yagyan' for 'Graha Shanti'. They believe if the first maturity occurred on Tuesday then it is called as 'Devidosha'. For this 'Devi dosha' they must do worship and 'yagyan' by sorcerer for the matured girl.

But in recent times the younger people have no such belief. They do not arrange any 'yagyan'. In case of death rituals various restriction are observed for ten days. But on tenth day they are become free from this pollution. All these customs that were prevailing in past, still continue in present. In death rituals all the customs are same. But now people do not believe the 'ekpa-dosha' and 'duipa-dosha' of the dead people.

CHANGES AMONG THE RELIGIOUS FUNCTIONARIES

Among Banjara, changes are also found in religious

functionaries. At first they were giving much respect to their Nayak or village headman. Then they were giving respect to village priest and sorcerer.

But now with the changing time these things are also changed. The respect for Nayak is still remaining same. But now they contact to the village priest only when they need or only at the time of worship. After that through out the year they do not contact to the priest. Earlier the sorcerer was very influential. But now people do not believe in such power or person as they do not have belief in any spirit. Now, only once or twice in a year they contact the 'Gunia' or Sorcerer.

They also now do not believe in such power of diviner or 'Bhagat'. A man of Dabriguda village said that, how is it possible for a Devi to be transmigrated to a person and that person can solve anything? It is only the false belief of the people. Besides all these things, now a days they believe there is no witch and witchcraft is not practiced in their village.

IMPACT OF EDUCATION

With the increase in education, modern thoughts are increasing slowly in an evolutionary manner among Banjara people. Some members have taken Dikhya. This is mainly due to the impact of modern educated. In Mushapalli village, there are four types of Dikhya members are found. They are Gayatri, Kalikrushna, Sannyashi Guru, and Baistav Guru.

Giridhari Naik, age 45, accepted the Gayatri Dikhya ten years ago. After that other villagers got influenced by seeing the restrictions of this Dikhya and started to become members of other such types of Dikhya.

In this Gayatri Dikhya the Giridhari does not take non-vegetarian food. He only takes vegetarian foods. He does not take liquor and also does not accept food from other house. He only takes foods from their Dikhya members' house. He puts a sacred thread on his body. He does meditation and utters sacred spells in a closed room every morning and evening. All the members of his family also observed all these restriction with him and they are also the members of Gayatri. This will give a kind of mental peace to him.

Beside that a person Chitrabhanu, age 50, of Mushapalli, who has taken 'Karna-mantra' from his Guru. The Guru is from Temera village. The person who takes 'Karna-mantra' put a white thread on his body and can do the worship of Brundabati, Danteswari, and Pedrani Devi. In this mantra he is given a training of how to worship deities. He does not take non-vegetarian food, liquor and all other alcoholic foods. He has to maintain a principled and orderly life.

EXCEPTIONAL CASE

I found an exceptional case in the context of conversion. Decades ago, in Hanspada village, a lady suffered from leprosy and all villager sex communicated her out of the village. The Christian missionary came to her rescue and treated her in the near by missionary medical center. Ultimately the girl was cured. She was also given proper education and given service in their missionary. On the back dropof social excommunication and isolation, it was enough for her to undergo conversion from Hinduism to Christianity.

9

CONCLUSION

A very famous definition given by Minian Smart says that, "there is no such thing as religion. There are customs, movements, persons, objects, sentiments, social groupings and so forth which are said to have religious or sacred characteristics, and there are organized systems of doctrine and practices which are commonly called religion."

So from time immemorial whenever a society started to develop, there are some institutions which are common to every society, these are political organization, economic organization, kinship organization and religious organization. All such institutions function in a holistic manner to make the social life comfortable, smooth and better every where around the world. However, since the dawn of human civilization man has been interacting with nature for aliving and is greatly dependent on the super naturalentities, where ever he fails to explain, achieve or face certain hazards of life. Thus, the religious organization has a great role in tribal society of banjara. So to have an analytical study on Banjara tribe of Kalahandi district, it tooks a time period 30 days. The Banjaras have also a great belief in supernatural entities. Their supernatural concepts are very much related to natural objects such as plants, flowers, animals, stone, sand and other things which they usually use in the rituals and consider as sacred objects. In their conceptualization of supernatural entities, they strongly go by gender factors. They are mostly devotees of Goddessess rather than Gods, even through they propitiate both. So to fulfill their wishes they also sacrifice different animals, offer fruits and flowers of different colours to the Goddesses. Besides the Goddesses of their culture, they also worship various Hindu deities mainly due to impact of long term acculturation. In Banjara society women are not allowed to actively take part in most of their worship, in some instances, they are not even allowed to witness the Puja. Only male members are allowed to do everything in Puja. So this shows they have a patrilineal society in which male members have the dominating position.

The Banjara people also celebrate communal rites and different festivals in various agricultural activities. These rites and festivals are observed to propitiate the supernatural entities so that they may get better and heal thier crops. During festivities, they individually observe Nabanna, Garvana Sankranti and Charu Puja, Tij, Pausa Purnima, Diwali, Holi are the communally observed festivals. These festivals and rituals provide a means for congregation.

In Banjara society the practices occuring during various festivals and worship are very strictly followed. The ritual practices mainly refers to actions, ceremonies, objects, art forms, music, charts etc., which are given a sacred significance and used to express religious sentiments and attitude.

In the birth, puberty, marriage and death rituals, the specific periods of pollution and impurity and the ways to become pure again are observed in a more rigid way than us. Unlike the birth and death events, marriage is accepted as a source of entertainment. In their society, they have only arranged marriages. Love marriage is not seen in their community. In Banjara society, when a girl gets her first menstrual cycle, they arrange a grand feast and observed pollution for six days and purifying rituals on seventh day. In birth and death, various restrictions are observed by them and purification is donein a grand ritualistic manner.

Religion is an important aspect of culture, so it acts as a cohesive in binding man together with the community and it also reflects the structure of the society. So by analyzing the religion of a society we can get a broad idea along with various informations on that society.

The Banjara people also have belief in animism. They believe in various types of soul and spirits. So the worship of dead ancestor spiritis found in their society. Though they are now accepting modern notions, the aged people among them still believe in different types of malevolent and benevolent spirit. The different malevolent spiritsare controlled by their religious specialist named by them as 'Guni'.

They also have belief in witchcraft. In their society the priest, Nayak, Diviner, Gunia, all have different roles. They give more respect to their religious specialists than to their magical specialist. In their society both religious and magical specialists are found. But now with the impact of modernization (especially through education and media awareness), their world view is changing. There is some good amount of difference in their thinking process. Now, they also do not believe in witchcraft and ghost, but in true sense, inspite of these changes, they'll never leave their tradition and customs.

The peripheral elements of their cultures are changing but the core elements which are mostly attached to religion are still found intact and have changed only to a little extent.

GLOSSARY

Amabasya	- New moon
anchal	- Dupatta
Arati	- A process during worship
Bani	- A ritual place to which they filled with sand
Barcha	- A pricking spear
Batabarna	- A ritual in marriage
Bauli	- Ornaments
Baunta	- Ornaments
Bhagaban	- God
Bhagat	- Devotee
Bhagirathi Cahaa	- Name of Banjara
Bhala	- Stick
Bhat	- Cement tumb which is worshipped as Danteswari
Bhukia	- A priest
Bihaghar	- Local term for marriage
Bijaya dashami	- Tenth day of Dussehra
Bindi	- a mark on females forehead
Chirangul	- spirit
Chittalagi Amabasya	- a festival on new moon

chuda - a kind of food
chudi - Bangles
Dakan - a typical witch craft
Dashami - Tenth day of Dusehra
Daskathia - Traditional dance by group of people
Datun - Stick which is used for cleaning teeth
Devata Ghara - The Goddess Room
Devi kheliba - Devi is transmigrated to the person who is carrying the symbol of Goddess.
Devir asana - The place of Devi
Dhaal - protective instrument
Dhai - Trained midwife
Dharam Devata - God
Dhoti - Traditional Male dress
Duguri - An object which is used for covering the footprint of Goddess
Duipa-dosha - Observed in death ritual
Dunguri - Well (which become filled with water after worshipping Swarga mailli)
Ekpa-dosha - Occured during death ritual
Gajamung - Ritual friendship
Gedi and Bhala - Ritual Stick
Ghagra - Dress of women
Gorous - cowdung solution
Gotra - clan
Gountia - A powerful family of Banjara village
Grahadhosha - The Astrosign i.e. defect in the planet
Grahashanti - A yagyan
Gudugudia - Spirit
Gunia - Sorcerer

Guru - Sorcerer
Handimar - Puberty
Hansli - Ornament
Hareliuansh - Festival
Hastha Ganthi - Tie the hands of both bride and groom during marriage
Holi - Festival of colours
Jalakamini - a Goddess
Kacheli - Blouse
Kad - a juice of gud, ghee, garlic, and a spices,
which is given to Banjara women
Kalash - Pot
Kalia Sar - a Black thread
Karna Mantra - Secretely spoken in ear
Khat - Bed
Kirtana - Singing and dancing on religious song
Madhusala - A specific room where newely married couple are kept
Maghapanchami - a special day for particular worship
Mahaprasad - A cooked food for makara which is prepared on the 9th day of death ritual
Mahaprasad - God's food
Makara - Ritual friend
Mala - Garland
Mana - A pot
Mangan - The day before marriage
Mashan pada - Burial ground
Mayurchandrika - a typical ornament decorated to bull
Mitthibat - a rice taken by dead person's family
Murda - Dead body

Nabani woods	- New wood
Nabanna	- Food prepared during festivals
Nakachana	- Fruits of particular plant
Nayak	- village chief
Okhara	- This is put in front of door and used mainly at newely married couple enter
Pagadi	- Turban
Panchamruta	- Mixture of ghee, jaggery, curd, honey and milk
Patala	- Underground
Pedrani devi Jatara	- Fair of the Goddess
Phagu	- a coloured powder
Phetua	- Female's dress
Pisacha	- Ghost
Pisacha	- spirit
Pitrupuja	- Worship Ancestors
Pitrupurusha	- Ancestor
Pitrusarat	- Given for mainting peace in house and dead ancestors
Pitrusarat	- It is an offering to old ancestors
Puja	- Worship
Pujari	- Priest
Rakhi purnima	- Tieing festival between sister and brother
Rakta bhoga	- Sacrificing animal to Banjara deities
Rashi oil	- Mustard oil
Ratha Yatra	- Chariot festival
Sagar	- Sea
Salwar	- Women's dress
Sapi	- Towel
Sarpanch	- Nayak or Village Head-man

Shanna	- Ritual cloth
Singli	- a typical ornament decorated to bull
Sukla bhoga	- a sacred food prepared on 1st day of Holi
Swarga	- Hevean
Tabij	- Locket
Talwar	- a kind of weapon
Thakura	- God
Thakurani Gudi	- a place of Goddess
Tulsi Plant	- Basil plant
Veranda	- Space in front of house

BIBLIOGRAPHY

Bohannan, Paul (1963), *Social Anthropology* (309-326), New York

Clark, Francis, William, Paul (1980), *The Religious Perspective and the Sense of the Holy*. The Open University Press, Walton Hall, Milton Keynes.

Douglas, Mary (1975), *Implicit meanings; essays in Anthropology*, London University Coll.

Eliade, Mircea (1987), *The Encyclopedia of Religion*, MacMillian Publishing Company, (p.380-390,422-443), New York.

Epstein, A.L (1967), *The Craft of Social Anthropology*, Tevistock Publication, London, (p.181-204 and p. 231-243) Oxford University Press.

Evans Pritchard, E.E. (1965), *Theories of Primitive.*

Fox, Robin (1975), *Encounter with Anthropology*, Britain

Friedl, Jhon (1981), *The Human Portrait. An International to Culture Anthropology*, Prentice-Hall.Inc

Friedle, John, Preifter E (1977), *Anthropology, The Study of People.* Harper and Raw Publishers, INC.

Gangte, T.S. (2002), Magico Religious Belief and Practices among Kukies, In *Man and Life*, (Jan-June), edited by P.K. Bhowmick.

Goode, William J. (1951), *Religion among Primitives*, New York.

Lessa, Willam A (1958), Reader in Comparative Religion, Havard University, New York.

Levistrauss, Claude (1969), *Structural Anthropology* (167-186), London

Mishra, J.D. (1977), *The World View of Indian Tribe in Tribal Heritage of India,* edited by S.C. Dube. Vikas Publication.

Murthy, ASN (1991), *Religion and Society, A Study of Koyas,* New Delhi.

Norbeck, Edward (1961), *Religion in Primitive Society,* New York

Oliver, Chand (1981), *The Discovery of Humanity.* Harper and Raw Publisher, (341-358), New York.

Russell, R.V. (1961), *The Tribes and Castes of the Central Provinces of India,* (Vol-4, festival), London.

Slotkin, J.S. (1950), *The Science of Human Society and Culture,* MacMillian Company, London.

INDEX